The Captain Departs

Ulysses S. Grant's Last Campaign

by Thomas M. Pitkin

With a Foreword by
John Y. Simon

SOUTHERN ILLINOIS UNIVERSITY PRESS
Carbondale and Edwardsville

Feffer & Simons, Inc.
London and Amsterdam

Library of Congress Cataloging in Publication Data

Pitkin, Thomas M
  The captain departs; Ulysses S. Grant's last
campaign.

  Bibliography: p.
  1. Grant, Ulysses Simpson, Pres. U.S., 1822–1885.
I. Title.
E672.P59   973.8′2′0924 [B]   73–4321
  ISBN 0–8093–0637–9

Printed in the United States of America
Designed by Gary Gore

The tumult and the shouting dies—
The captains and the kings depart.
Kipling, "Recessional"

Contents

List of Illustrations

Foreword

EARLY IN 1885 Americans learned that General Ulysses S. Grant was writing his memoirs in a desperate race for time against an incurable cancer. For six months newspaper readers followed the dramatic contest, and the hearts of Americans were touched by the general's last battle. Not all had sympathized with his plight one year earlier, when the swindles of Ferdinand Ward had left the Grant family destitute, for there was room for criticism of the ex-president's involvement with Wall Street, and of his great naïveté which furthered Ward's simple theft. Yet all could sympathize with the great bond of family affection which drove Grant on, despite excruciating pain, to leave some support for his family.

Grant first gave the American people reason for identification with him during the Civil War when he led his armies with a refreshing lack of military show. Rarely in full uniform, never brandishing his sword to lead a charge, and always conscious of the painful costs of war, Grant impressed his fellow Americans as a satisfyingly unmilitary general. Resilience, resistance to outside pressure, and receptivity to innovation—common traits carried to their heights—were the marks of his generalship. Accepting both victory and defeat with the same equanimity, he pursued a dogged course toward peace. At Appomattox and afterward he showed a deep desire for genuine reconciliation of North and South.

The unmilitary general was also an unpolitical president. He pursued an independent course, thought through his decisions carefully, and paid little attention to his critics. Though less successful in the White House than on the battlefield, most Americans could credit him with trying, and his last message to Congress contained something of an apology for mistakes. Stubbornness and errors in judgment of men, his most notable flaws, were again common traits. Years after leaving the White House he made his first political speech.

The victorious general of the Civil War, the youngest man elected president until the twentieth century—then triumphantly reelected—never lost touch with the simple realities of American life. Devoted to his family, loyal to his friends, and ordinary in manner and appearance, his character combined elements extremely simple and extraordinarily complex. "What an illustration," marveled Walt Whitman, "of the capacities of that American individuality common to us all."

President Lincoln had died with shattering suddenness in an assassination dramatically timed and under circumstances encouraging the development of legend and myth. Grant, however, faded away in a manner sadly familiar to many American families. He accepted the inevitable with quiet courage, and the battle to finish his memoirs once more roused the Grant of Shiloh and Vicksburg. Though grateful for research and secretarial assistance, he was determined to compose the book himself; for Grant, there was no other way.

Under the circumstances, it was victory enough that the *Memoirs* were completed; their remarkable quality made them a triumph. Grant once again displayed the modesty, equanimity, and fairness which were his characteristics, and added a surprising sense of humor and literary ability. Matthew Arnold, the English critic, who had once met Grant and found him uninteresting, through the *Memoirs* now met a man of admirable character. Though the language lacked "high breeding," he found it "straightforward, nervous, firm, possessing in general the high merit of saying clearly in the fewest possible words what had to be said, and saying it, frequently, with shrewd and unexpected turns of expression." Mark Twain took angry exception to Arnold's remarks concerning Grant's grammar, and went on to praise the *Memoirs* as "something which will still bring to American ears, as long as America shall last, the roll of his vanished drums and the tread of his marching hosts."

Grant's last year, then, was one of both personal and literary triumph in the midst of tragedy. It has long deserved careful scholarly attention both for what it reveals about a great American hero and about the people who considered him heroic. Though told without maudlin touches, the story will still leave few emotionally uninvolved, for it is an account of pain and suffering as well as mighty deeds, and truly deserves to be considered the general's final victory.

John Y. Simon
Executive Director
Ulysses S. Grant Association

Carbondale, Illinois
January 1973

Preface

THIS STUDY of the last year in the life of General Ulysses S. Grant is the outgrowth of a report on the Grant cottage at Mount McGregor, New York, prepared for the Office of State History, New York State Education Department, at the instance of Mr. Horace Willcox, Principal Museum Curator. Little research had been done on the site, which is owned by the state and kept open to the public, and a broad general study was needed as an aid to interpretive planning.

The draft was submitted for review to Dr. John Y. Simon, of the Ulysses S. Grant Association at Southern Illinois University, editor of *The Papers of Ulysses S. Grant,* now in progress. Dr. Simon, after noting a few necessary corrections, expressed the belief that the report made a contribution to the literature on General Grant. He suggested that it be revised and amplified with further research, with a view to publication. The Office of State History gave its blessing to such a project. As I have had opportunity, I have since done a very considerable amount of fresh research, and have expanded and revised the original report. Much new material, some of it relatively unused, has been woven into the text. Here and there is not only amplification but also modification of the original thesis.

The final year of Grant's life, after a period of relative calm and obscurity, was one of drama, triumph, and tragedy. He became once more a conspicuous public figure as his struggle with sudden adversity and malignant disease developed. Bankrupted by an unscrupulous partner in Wall Street, he set out to recoup his fortunes and those of his family by writing his recollections of the Civil War. Just launched on this enterprise, he was stricken by cancer. The remaining months of his life were a desperate and agonizing struggle to complete the book before he died. The whole nation watched the drama as it unfolded. Grant's last days in New York City and on Mount McGregor, filled with pain and heroic effort at an unaccustomed but absorbing task, were followed with eager interest, growing sympathy, and admiration. The voices of his numerous enemies were stilled, and when he died, his task accomplished, there was universal mourning.

Along with the main thread of the narrative, there are woven subsidiary themes with their own interest. The effort to make Mount McGregor, a fine scenic area not far from Saratoga Springs, into a paying summer resort reached its climax with Grant's stay on the mountain and his death there in the summer of 1885. The contest between the Century Company, which had started the general writing, and Mark Twain for publication rights to the general's book, was an interesting and sometimes amusing affair. Twain's own effort to help the general finish the book, when he found on his hands a dying author who was also a good friend, is a warmly human story. The personal animosities that developed among those close to the old hero, to whom they were all individually devoted, and the note of greed that was struck as the smell of money began to rise from the book venture, are instructive.

The success of the *Personal Memoirs of U. S. Grant* as a publication was astonishing. There had never been anything quite like it in American publishing history. The general did not live to see it, but he knew before he died that his beloved wife would never be in want, and that relatives who had shared his losses in Wall Street would be provided for. He had fought off pain and death to some purpose, but to the point of exhaustion, adding one more splendid victory to those of his military career. There was nothing left worth struggling for. Still read today, the work is a model of straightforward dramatic narrative, covering the events of a tremendous epoch in American history. It remains perhaps the greatest of all monuments to the man who, with Lincoln, preserved the United States intact.

The cottage in which Grant completed the *Personal Memoirs* and died, on the top of Mount McGregor, was preserved by its owner and the general's old comrades of the Grand Army of the Republic. It was finally taken over by the State of New York, and is maintained for public inspection as one of its distinguished group of historic sites. The removal to another site of the Wilton School for retarded children, which now physically overshadows it, is in prospect. The opportunity to make the whole mountaintop into a splendid small state park combining historic and recreational interest lies open.

Thomas M. Pitkin

New York City
January 1973

The Captain Departs

1. General Grant Becomes an Author

AFTER LEAVING the White House in 1877, following his two terms as president, General Ulysses S. Grant made a grand tour of the world. He was received as an honored guest by crowned heads and presidents. It was a triumphal and spectacular journey, but it was expensive and funds ran low. His second son, Ulysses, Jr., had made investments for his father, however, the profits of which permitted the general and Mrs. Grant, after a lengthy stay in Europe, to complete their travels by way of India, China, and Japan. They returned to the United States through San Francisco in 1879.[1]

The Grants were then making their home in Galena, Illinois, but they had acquired tastes which could not well be indulged there, and they felt prosperous enough to move to a more stirring and sophisticated setting. There was a final fling in politics, with Grant's friend, Senator Roscoe Conkling of New York, in 1880 leading a group of "Stalwarts" in a hopeless effort to secure his nomination to a third term on the Republican ticket. After its failure, the general and Mrs. Grant decided to move to New York City. There young Ulysses, not long out of Columbia University law school, had become the junior partner of a financier by the name of Ferdinand Ward, whose spectacular and apparently successful operations soon gave him the name of the "Young Napoleon of finance." It was investments with Ward and his associate James D. Fish that had financed the latter part of the general's world tour. Ward now proposed a private banking firm under the name of Grant & Ward. Grant and his son contributed their limited resources to the firm, and young Ulysses's father-in-law, Senator Jerome B. Chaffee of Colorado, invested heavily. Other members and connections of the family were drawn in, and the firm seemed for some time to be a fabulous success. In three years it acquired a rating of $15,000,000.[2]

Grant was never actively engaged in the affairs of this banking and brokerage house. His name was used, and he invested his money, but the business was almost entirely in Ward's hands. Ward made the investments, drew the checks, received the deposits and disposed of them. The company seemed to be making enormous profits, and the general had complete confidence in his young partner. He was relieved from the fear or the reality of poverty that had haunted much of his earlier life. "At last," as his grandson has phrased it, "he could enjoy his comfortable home, filled with the trophies acquired during a successful career in the army, the presidency and during the trip around the world. Also he could now meet on a basis of social equality with the wealthy and socially prominent people who were proud to claim his acquaintance."[3] Early in 1884 the general felt affluent enough to start a round robin subscription toward the Statue of Liberty pedestal fund, offering $5,000 on condition that nineteen other prominent men did the same.[4]

While Grant thought that he was becoming a wealthy man through his partnership with Ward, his active interest lay elsewhere. He had shown himself a warm friend to Mexico after the Civil War, when he had sent a strong force to the border under General Philip Sheridan to lend moral support and suggest possible intervention to the legitimate government of Mexico in its struggle with the French and their puppet emperor, Maximilian. He had met and befriended Matias Romero, the Mexican representative in the United States at the time. Early in 1880 he went to Mexico and renewed his friendship with Romero. He was given a royal welcome and became enthusiastic over the possibilities of development in that country, to the mutual benefit of Mexico and American investors.[5]

After his political career ended, the general became an active propagandist for closer ties with Mexico, and took part in the promotion of railroads to develop the country's resources and link it more closely with the United States. The Mexican Southern Railroad Company was incorporated under the laws of New York State early in 1881 to build a line from Mexico City south. Grant and Romero, with Porfirio Diaz and other Mexican gentlemen, were listed as incorporators, along with Edwin D. Morgan, Jay Gould, Russell Sage, Jesse Seligman, Collis P. Huntington, and other American financiers and railroad operators. Grant became the president of the company and set up an office at 2 Wall Street, the same address as that of Grant & Ward. Here, after another trip to Mexico to promote a concession from the government, he spent most of his time seeking to raise the funds for construction.[6]

Like many another organization with an imposing letterhead, the Mexican Southern Railroad Company seems to have had few working members. Contributions came in slowly. John Bigelow, a well-known diplomat, writer, and editor, warned against investment in Mexican railroads in an article in *Harper's Magazine,* affirming in effect "that the money invested in railroads in Mexico will not pay a reasonable interest, and that therefore it is not safe to make such investments." Romero, then the Mexican minister to the United States, took issue publicly with Bigelow, thereby calling attention to the article and probably adding to the damage done. At the same time a slow depression began developing in the United States, accompanied by increasing labor unrest. It was not a favorable climate for foreign investment. Serious construction work was never begun on the Mexican Southern, and the Mexican government eventually canceled the concession for lack of performance. Grant and Romero had meanwhile been appointed commissioners by their respective governments to draft a reciprocity treaty. This treaty, which would have placed railroad equipment and other American machinery on the Mexican free list, was finally ratified by the Senate, but with an amendment making it inoperative pending the passage of supporting legislation. This legislation was not forthcoming and the treaty was, in effect, stillborn.[7]

These were serious disappointments to General Grant, but he still considered himself a wealthy man in the spring of 1884. Friends in the financial world had tried to caution him about the highly unorthodox business practices of his firm under Ward's management, but he refused to listen. Where Grant had once given his trust, he was hard to move. It was a trait in his character that had brought him trouble before. On May 6 the Marine National Bank, of which Fish was president, closed its doors. Grant & Ward a few hours later announced their suspension. When the general reached his office at noon, his son told him that he had better go home; that the bank had failed. Grant took it quietly, but stayed in the office awhile and soon afterward told a close friend, who had dropped in to see him, "We are all ruined here." Ward had disappeared, he said. The securities of the firm were locked up in the safe, and only Ward had the key. He refused to discuss the matter with inquiring reporters, telling them quietly but decisively: "I've nothing to say. I don't want to talk about it." He soon left for his home on 66th Street.[8]

The news that the Marine Bank had failed and that Grant & Ward had suspended operations caused a sensation in Wall Street. Other failures a few days later brought the threat of a real panic, which was averted only by the prompt action of a number of conservative bankers. It was quickly learned that the ex-president and his son were involved in the misfortunes of Grant & Ward, and there were expressions of sympathy on every hand. Grant was probably unfamiliar with the details of the business, friendly newspapers noted, and thought it very profitable even when it was on the verge of failure. Ferdinand Ward, it was said, had dragged the firm down by his extensive real estate speculations with Fish. When it was learned that Ward was a director of Fish's bank, and that Fish was a special partner in Grant & Ward, the two failures were quickly linked. It was thought at first that Grant & Ward had been carried down by the failure of the Marine Bank. A later story was that the bank's suspension was due to its transactions with that firm. "The house was never rated among the strong ones," the *New*

York Tribune said, "and of late its operations have excited suspicion as to its financial condition." Ugly rumors of embezzlement were soon afloat.[9]

Ward soon came out of hiding and went into conference with his counsel. He was at once put under surveillance by clamorous creditors. Fraud on his part and that of Fish quickly became apparent. The court appointed a receiver for Grant & Ward, and the controller of the currency a receiver for the Marine Bank. At an early hearing, Ward admitted making false entries in the accounts of Grant & Ward. He said that his partners knew little about the firm's operations, which had been mainly personal; "that he simply borrowed from Peter to pay Paul"; and that he had been trying to avoid insolvency in this way for two years. He appeared near collapse and was excused for the time from further testimony. A grand jury was called to look into the whole matter. Several lawsuits were quickly launched, but without much hope of recovery in the case of Grant & Ward investors. The receiver, after a preliminary investigation, estimated the firm's liabilities at over $16,000,000 and its actual assets at $57,000. Some angry creditors applied for an order of arrest against members of the firm, including the general himself, but were denied by the court.[10]

Ward had ruined the whole Grant family, Colonel Frederick D. Grant, the general's oldest son, told reporters. The business had been very lucrative at first, and he had been induced to invest his capital along with that of his brother. "Ward ran the business and was trusted by us all. What we are going to do is uncertain. My father is ruined like the rest of us, and is equally uncertain as to the future." Henry Clews, a leading Wall Street figure and a good friend of the general's, said later that Grant was a victim of his lack of early training in financial business. It had happened to him as it had happened to others who had been successful in other lines and thought they could be equally successful in the Street. Grant was a highly successful soldier; he was no financier. "The great captain of the Union's salvation," Clews affirmed, "was as helpless as a babe when Ferdinand Ward and James D. Fish moved upon his works." [11]

There were those that questioned Grant's innocence. The New York *Sun,* long his bitter opponent, led the attack. Officials of the Marine National Bank, under heavy fire, said they had believed mistakenly that the firm of Grant & Ward was making enormous amounts of money out of government contracts secretly obtained through the influence of General Grant. Fish had correspondence with Grant, which he circulated privately in photographic copies, indicating that Grant had given him assurance on the point. Grant's attorneys were forced, in his defense, to release the whole correspondence to the press. The only letter in Grant's handwriting to Fish referred to another matter entirely. Ward had, they said, prepared another brief letter to Fish for Grant's signature and the general had signed it without question, thinking that it was a matter of mere business routine. Ward himself much later admitted that this was the case, but the immediate effect was damaging. The letter contained language that could be interpreted in a damning way: "I think the investments are safe, and I am willing that Mr. Ward should derive what profit he can for the firm that the use of my name and influence may bring." "Is Ulysses S. Grant Guilty?" the *Sun* trumpeted editorially. Fish, it said, had been "misled by the written word of a man who has twice been chosen President of the United States, and whose name is one of the most famous in the military history of modern times." The Fish-Grant correspondence, it charged, showed that "For the love of money the greatest military reputation of our time has been dimmed and degraded by its possessor. The people look on with shame." Actually, as Ward confessed long afterward when he was in prison, Fish and he had cooked up the correspondence with the deliberate purpose of convincing possible investors that Grant & Ward did have profitable government contracts and that Grant not only knew and approved of this but had used his influence to get them. These contracts, of course, never existed.[12]

Grant had long experience of scurrilous personal attacks, but the shock of business failure had been a severe one and the reflections on his personal honesty were mortifying. Even more distressing to him was the knowledge that others, depending on his name, had invested in Grant & Ward and had been fleeced. Most embarrassing was a personal debt to William H. Vanderbilt that he had contracted on the very eve of the disaster. Ward had called on him on May 4, and represented to him that the Marine Bank was in temporary difficulties. It needed $150,000 at once for only one day, until it could call in loans. Grant & Ward had over $600,000 to their credit in the bank at that time, he assured the general, besides $1,300,000 of unpledged securities in their own vaults. These resources, it developed later, were practically nonexistent. Grant had gone to Vanderbilt and been given a personal check for $150,000, "not," as Vanderbilt explained later, "because it was business like, but simply because the request came from Gen. Grant." [13]

Vanderbilt tried in every way to cancel the debt, but both the general and Mrs. Grant refused to accept his generosity. This was a personal obligation, they insisted, not to be canceled by any bankruptcy proceedings in the case of Grant & Ward, and Grant was determined to meet it. He turned over to Vanderbilt practically all his property, including real estate and his swords, medals, and other trophies of the Civil War, together with the lavish gifts that had been given him by admirers all over the world. Mrs. Grant finally accepted the return of the trophies, on agreement that they should go in perpetual trust to the government. General William T. Sherman and wealthy friends had been trying to raise a fund to relieve the general's distress, and "to prevent his war relics from falling into strange hands." Grant had firmly refused to accept such a fund, and they now desisted, hoping for some action in Congress toward placing him on the army retired list.[14]

Both Ward and Fish were soon indicted, and both went to prison for long terms, but the Grant family had been impoverished. They had been the victims of a "shrewd and ingratiating adventurer," Hamlin Garland says, who had carried on for years an extraordinary game of bluff, "a stupendous scheme of paying profits from a principal which was never invested or which went to pay some clamorous debtor"; it was "a

*Panic scene in Wall Street a few days after the failure of Grant &
Ward. Ferdinand Ward and Grant opened a private banking firm
in the early 1880s, and within three years it had a rating of
$15,000,000 before it collapsed from Ward's rascality on May 6,
1884. Illustration is from* Harper's Weekly, May 24, 1884.—
Courtesy of The New-York Historical Society, New York City

blind pool into which he led men to their ruin and ultimately to his own ruin." But if Grant and his family were naïve in being taken in by Ward, so were many more experienced in the world of finance. Ward's methods constituted a huge confidence game. "He had the art of dissembling in great perfection," a Wall Street veteran commented, "and was possessed of extraordinarily persuasive powers, without appearing to have any selfish object in view." Some of the richest financiers became his victims, "chiefly induced by promises of high rates of interest and large profits on various ventures." [15]

It took the court-appointed receiver two years of hard work to prepare a final report on the affairs of Grant & Ward, and even then there were mysteries. Ward had carried on the business of the firm almost alone, the report said. Other partners were called in only occasionally on individual deals. Accounts were fragmentary and unreliable; many entries did not represent actual transactions, but were made by the bookkeeper at Ward's direction. He had carried on most of the firm's business in his own name, and mingled his personal affairs freely with it. Moneys had been received for which there were no entries, and he had paid out large sums of money of which no entries had been made in the firm's ledgers. Substantially from the organization of the firm his practice had been to rehypothecate securities, that is, to use securities placed on deposit with the firm as collateral to raise new loans, "depositing the proceeds of loans on them in his own bank accounts." [16]

In the fall of 1880, when it became clear that Grant's political career was at an end, a group of his admirers, led by George E. Jones of the *New York Times,* had subscribed a trust fund of $250,000 for him. This was at first referred to in the promotion as the "Presidential Retiring Fund," of which Grant was to be merely the first beneficiary. But it was found that only the magic of Grant's name would produce subscriptions, and the fund became one frankly for his benefit. It was invested largely in railroad bonds, producing an income of approximately $15,000 a year. This resource remained to the general after the failure of Grant & Ward, as the *Sun* was careful to point out, but it, too, soon disappeared as the railroad defaulted on its bonds.[17]

It was in this situation that the editors of *Century Magazine* approached the general with renewed pleas to contribute to its series of articles on the Civil War by participants. When the series was in the early planning stage a few months before, General Grant had naturally been the first prospective contributor approached. But he had seemed indifferent to his past career and referred the *Century* people to Adam Badeau's three-volume *Military History of U. S. Grant,* saying "It is all in Badeau." "His declination was so decisive," Robert U. Johnson, associate editor of the magazine in charge of the war series, recalled later, "that it left us without hope." [18]

A few weeks after the failure of Grant & Ward, Johnson renewed the attempt through Badeau, who was known as a close personal friend of the general's and had been asked to use his influence in the earlier approach. Johnson called attention to the general sympathy upon Grant's misfortune, and suggested that the public would welcome the publication of material by him "concerning a part of his honored career in which every one takes pride." It might be that Grant would welcome diversion from his troubles. Badeau, who had recently resigned his consular appointment in Havana, was already negotiating with *Century Magazine* on a proposed article about the general. Grant appeared at first reluctant, but soon after changed his mind. The Society of the Army of the Potomac held its annual reunion in Brooklyn on June 11, and Grant was elected as its president in a scene of great enthusiasm. He came to the reunion in person to accept the appointment, hobbling on crutches from an accident of the winter before, and the ovation he received must have been heartwarming. The *Century* editors at the time were rather discouraged about their efforts to line up leading generals to contribute to their war series, scheduled to start that fall, and were seriously considering postponing it another year. Richard Watson Gilder, senior editor of the Century Company, saw a ray of hope in the Brooklyn episode. "Grant's recent election to the Army of the Potomac position may reengage his attention to military matters," he wrote Johnson. "He must be; this is [our] strongest hold." Soon after, to their "surprise and joy," the editors received a note from the general saying that, if they still desired to have him write for the war series, he would be glad to have them send someone to discuss the matter.[19]

Grant was then at Long Branch, New Jersey, where he had maintained a summer cottage for many years. Johnson was spending the summer at a nearby point on the Jersey coast, and at once called upon the general. So began an association that he recalled later as "one of the fortunate experiences of my life, since it revealed to me the heroism and the integrity of a much misrepresented man." As Johnson remembered the interview years later, Grant, before he would discuss the proposed articles, spent fifteen minutes explaining to Johnson in detail his association with Ward and the situation in which the recent failure had left him. Johnson was surprised and honored by these confidences. The general admitted that "his changed financial condition had compelled him to consider what resources might be offered by his pen." He had arrived at Long Branch almost penniless. He asked how many articles the *Century* could use, if it should prove that he could write at all, and Johnson assured him that they could use as many as he could write. However, their impression was that he could cover the ground of his own major campaigns in four articles—on Shiloh, Vicksburg, the Wilderness, and Lee's surrender. Grant agreed and said that he would start on Shiloh at once.[20]

Actually, these things did not all happen at one interview. Johnson, in his book of reminiscences, *Remembered Yesterdays*, condensed a number of meetings with Grant. He was at Long Branch several times that summer. He did at least get Grant started writing at the first interview, and a draft on Shiloh arrived in the *Century* office on July 1. The editors were jubilant. Grant's participation in the war series gave a tremendous boost to the project. "Hurrah for Grant. Now for Sheridan & Sherman!" So Gilder wrote Johnson as soon as he got the word. "Gen. Grant on 'Shiloh' is *decisive* and soldierly but not picturesque. Hurrah!" This was the comment of Clarence C. Buel, Johnson's associate in the war series, on first seeing the manuscript. Johnson at once began thinking of a book. The Century Company was already planning a large book on the Civil War, to follow and incorporate the series of articles. "Now that Grant is in the humor of writing," he suggested to Gilder, "would it not be worth while to think of getting him to write a book of his war experiences for subscription to go along side of our book? . . ." [21]

After the excitement of getting Grant to write for their series at all had died down, the *Century* editors realized that his article on Shiloh was essentially a copy of his official report of the action, with which they were already familiar. It had none of the color and personal anecdote that they particularly wanted. Grant had no idea of the needs of a popular publication on the war. Johnson set about tactfully coaching him, and found him an apt pupil. When he realized that what was wanted was not a cold, objective report but his personal account, with his point of view, with everything that concerned him, with what he planned, thought, saw, said, and did, it was a revelation. He took back the rejected copy and rewrote it completely. The result was a highly successful article, Grant's first conscious literary effort, that appeared in the *Century* in February 1885. [22]

The general soon began to enjoy the work. It not only diverted him from his financial troubles but gave him the satisfaction of finding that he could do something new. The next article for the *Century* series was to be on Vicksburg. On July 15 he wrote Johnson, "I have now been writing on the Vicksburg Campaign two weeks, Sundays and all, averaging more than four hours a day. Only now approaching Champion Hill, I fear that my article will be longer than you want." [23] Once the flood of wartime recollection was loosed, it was hard to stop.

The idea of persuading Grant to write a book developed quickly. Gilder passed on Johnson's suggestion at once to Roswell Smith, the president of the Century Company, and Smith approved. "I think well of the project of a subscription book by Genl. Grant on the war," he told Gilder. If the business office thought it would sell, he said, "we may as well secure it at once." No sooner had the idea taken hold among the Century people than they began to realize that other publishers might forestall them. "Grant's book *in our hands,*" Gilder wrote the office from his summer home, "would be better matter more anecdotal, complete & probably more correct & valuable than in some other hands. (Johnson has already improved, by his suggestions, the first article by Grant.) I do not see how it could fail to attract attention throughout the world." Johnson soon discovered that Grant was ahead of them. On July 22 he wrote Gilder that he had spent all morning with the general, discussing Shiloh, Vicksburg, and projected papers on the Wilderness and Lee's surrender. The first draft on Vicksburg was nearing completion. Grant's good friend and summer neighbor, George W. Childs of the *Public Ledger,* and other Philadelphia friends, "one of whom is a publisher," Johnson reported to Gilder in some alarm, had been urging him to write a book on his campaigns. He "had already formed the intention" of doing it the next winter. "Nothing was said however about publication & he said that he would not publish it without letting us have a chance." [24]

At about the same time a Long Branch correspondent of the *Baltimore American* sent in a letter telling of a visit to Grant at his cottage. "I found the General in his library among a mass of papers and books, hard at work on his history of the siege of Vicksburg, one of a series of works on the civil war which when finished will doubtless give to the world an impartial and thorough history of that great epoch in our nation's life." The general told him a funny story about the siege and laughed heartily. The visitor was glad to find him in such a cheerful mood, "as his late business troubles must have worried him considerably." When Grant had completed the several accounts of campaigns, the writer understood, he would "connect the different engagements into one complete résumé of the 'little difficulty.' " In his labors he was assisted by his son, Colonel Fred Grant, "whose varied experience makes him a valuable companion." The writer had no doubt that, when finished, "the book will be in great demand and will add largely to his revenues." Gilder was annoyed by this story. Some reporter had told what Grant was doing, he wrote Johnson, "& steals an anecdote (but don't mention our name). Grant will have to be on his guard & not give away his material." [25]

By the middle of August it was clearly understood at the Century Company that Grant was going to write a book, the only question being as to whether they were going to publish it. Badeau came in and confirmed this. "Evidently the firm which is willing to pay down is going to get the book," Buel reported. Colonel Grant came in the same day and brought the revised Vicksburg article, asking for the check so that he could send it to his father. It was now decided that the next Grant article was to be on Chattanooga, evidently in place of Appomattox. "By this we get more of him early in the series," Gilder told Johnson. "It wont hurt our book to have him use the articles (even as they appear with us) in his book. We claim the 'combination' and the pictures. I should think his book would be a first rate 'spec' and even if it didn't prove a great financial success it would greatly advertise the house that published it." [26]

Gilder wrote to Grant's good friend Childs, "asking him to say a good word for the Century Co. to U. S. G. so that he would give us *the refusal* of his book." The editorial staff were all eager to have the Grant book, but Roswell Smith, who was summering in Saratoga but was to meet the general in September, had become cautious. Buel wrote him that the book wasn't as much of a speculation as it seemed. He argued that it would complement the articles. The material as it appeared in the magazine "would help to keep up our 'boom' with the soldier audience, and it would still have vitality—as a subscription book." Grant had no other income at the moment than the $500 apiece for the *Century* articles, he told Smith. Johnson telegraphed Smith shortly afterward, evidently suggesting advances to Grant, but Smith wrote Gilder that in his reply "I said we do not want Grant's book unless he wants us to have it, nor unless terms are equitable. I said bad policy for author to accept advances, but would make advances if need be on completion &c." He thought that Gilder and Johnson could do better with Grant and Childs than he could.[27]

Gilder urged the Grant book on Smith more than once before the latter returned to New York at the end of the summer. "Mr. Johnson understands the book situation, evidently with thoroughness," he told Smith late in August. "If we take it, it would be good for the book to announce its appearance in England, France & Germany—simultaneously." He thought Grant would like that. They ought to use all of the book possible in the magazine, "so long as a good portion is reserved for the book itself. We have never had such a card before as Grant, let alone the other papers in the series." Two days later he wrote again, repeating to Smith his belief that Grant was the most "taking" card that Century had ever had. "With all his faults & shortcomings he continues to be the most eminent and interesting of living Americans." He thought that they could hardly have too much of him in the magazine, and "the book, especially as it would be framed in our hands, would be a most important contribution to human history—a book, 'not for a day but for all time.' " [28]

Early in September, Smith went with Johnson to Long Branch, where they had been invited to luncheon with the general by Mr. Childs. Later they walked over to the Grant cottage. As they sat on the veranda discussing the book project, Johnson recalled later, Grant naïvely asked Smith, "Do you really think anyone would be interested in a book by me?" Smith replied, "General, do you not think the public would read with avidity Napoleon's personal account of his battles?" Such heavy flattery was hardly necessary at this point. Grant had found a new medium of expression, he saw a way of making some money for his family, and only physical force could have prevented him from writing a book. A day or two later Smith wrote Gilder, saying that the meeting with Grant had been "in every way satisfactory, and I think a good impression was made on both sides." He found Grant well informed on the subscription book business, "and very much disgusted with the way in which it is normally managed." He did not propose to pay a scalawag canvasser $6 for selling a $12 book not worth more than half the money, mentioning a case of this sort. "His ideas agree with ours—to make a good book, manufacture it handsomely, sell it at a reasonable price and make it so commanding that we can secure competent agents at a fair commission." The day had been a charming one and the interview a very memorable pleasure. "When the book is ready he is to come to us with it." [29]

The next day Gilder wrote to Johnson, asking him to thank Smith for his interesting letter about the visit to Grant. "I think he must have seen that the President of the Century Co. would be a good man to 'tieup' to as a publisher." Grant had, indeed, been impressed, but felt that he had made no commitment. A few days later he wrote Badeau, noting that Roswell Smith had been at Long Branch to see him. There would be no difficulty about the publication, he said, if the Century Company were to be the publishers. "My own opinion is that they would be the best publishers. But I will make no committal until about the time for publication." Obviously, Smith had offered no advance, although he was well informed of Grant's poverty. Desperately as he needed the money, Grant had probably been too proud to mention the matter. He had "just finished Chattanooga," he informed Badeau, and was next going to complete the work "up to where the Wilderness Campaign begins, and then go back to the beginning." Evidently he meant the beginning of his life; he was going to start an autobiography before completing the articles. When the Grant family got back to New York, he said, he would have a room for Badeau where he would always be welcome. As soon as they were settled, he would like to have Badeau go over with him "the remaining articles for the *Century.*" [30]

Badeau had been helping the general in his new field of endeavor, and was to continue to do so. How much this assistance amounted to eventually became a matter of bitter controversy. Badeau naturally made the most of it, as Grant's *Personal Memoirs* became a highly spectacular success, while the Grant family as naturally minimized it. Badeau had been the general's military secretary during the final campaigns of the Civil War and later. When he undertook his military history, Grant had made available to him the carefully kept and voluminous papers of his wartime headquarters. Badeau had used these as his basic sources, but prepared his own maps and added other material. Grant had long ago made his military secretary a brevet brigadier general, and had later given him splendid consular appointments while it was in his power to do so. He considered Badeau a personal friend, and had attached him to his party while traveling in Europe. Grant had great respect for his literary ability and, at first, little or no confidence in his own. Now Badeau, having quarreled with his superiors, was out of a job. It was entirely natural that Grant should call on him for help.[31]

Badeau was living out of the city, completing his own article on Grant for the *Century* and planning a novel, when the general called him to Long Branch to show him the first draft of the Shiloh article. Badeau was evidently a little annoyed, perhaps a bit contemptuous. "We worked it over together," he recalled later, "and when it was, as he thought, complete, he sent it to the editors." This draft Grant rewrote later, under Johnson's coaching. Johnson says that his office sent Badeau a copy of the proof. Badeau "made a few single-word corrections of no importance, such as 'received' for 'got'—by no means an improvement on the General's Saxon style." Johnson grew proud of his association with Grant, and no doubt felt that his coaching was all the help needed. Badeau and he inevitably became rivals. Grant in the first days of his literary apprenticeship unquestionably welcomed all the professional assistance he could get. His son Fred helped him, too, probably from the beginning, and stayed with him until the end. Pride of authorship was a slow growth.[32]

Badeau also had a look at the Vicksburg draft while it was in progress. When a rough draft, on which Johnson had been coaching him, was completed, Grant asked Badeau to come to Long Branch and spend at least a week. The general told him when he arrived that he intended to write a book and wanted Badeau's assistance. "I stayed ten days at his house," Badeau says, "planning the entire work with him, revising once more what he had written about Vicksburg and Shiloh, and mapping out what was yet to be done with the articles on Chattanooga and the Wilderness for the *Century Magazine*." Grant made him a formal offer for his help, though he wanted it kept strictly secret, and Badeau accepted.[33]

When Grant told Badeau about the interview with Smith in September, he assured him that there would always be a room for him at the house in town. Early in October the Grant family were settled there and the general renewed the offer. He had finished the Wilderness article before leaving Long Branch, he said, and intended to go to work on the book in a few days, "and to continue busily until I am done." Badeau was then working on a novel with a Cuban setting, which was to show up the incompetence and corruption in the State Department under President Arthur's administration. He wanted to get it published before Arthur left office, and was reluctant to leave off. Grant urged him again and Badeau went. Grant had fitted up a small room at the head of the stairs as a workroom, with a table and a large desk. "The 'small room at the head of the stairs,' " Badeau said later, "was that in which he wrote the greater part of his Personal Memoirs. The articles for *The Century* were remade there, and all the biographical part of the first volume, the story of the Mexican war, the beginning of his military career, indeed all of the work down to the Wilderness Campaign, and even the first draft of that—all were written and revised in that room, with me sitting by his side." [34]

Samuel L. Clemens, better known as "Mark Twain," and Grant had become good friends. They were probably the two best-known Americans of the day, and they had formed a sort of little mutual admiration society. When Twain was in New York from his home in Hartford, he often called on the general to smoke a cigar and talk. Twain, having quarreled with one publisher after another, had recently set up his own publishing house, in partnership with his niece's husband, under the name of Charles L. Webster & Co. In the summer and fall of 1884 they were preparing to publish as their first venture, on subscription, *The Adventures of Huckleberry Finn*. Some years before, when William Dean Howells had asked Mark's help in saving his father's consular appointment, they had come to New York and had lunch with Grant. At that time, Twain remembered later, "I tried hard . . . to get General Grant to agree to write his memoirs for publication." Grant would not listen to his suggestion. He was diffident; he had no confidence in his ability to write well; he was sure that the book would have only a humiliatingly small sale; and he needed no addition to his income. All Twain's arguments were wasted.[35]

In November 1884, Twain, who had been on a lecture tour, learned by accident from Richard Watson Gilder that Grant had written three articles for *Century,* was preparing a fourth, and was going to go on and write his memoirs in full. The Century Company was paying Grant $500 apiece for the articles, Gilder said, and he had been gratified at his first check. Mark was astonished; he had no idea that Grant was so poor that such a price would be attractive to him. Further, to his mind it was an insult. In his opinion, $10,000 would have been a trivial sum to offer the general. The whole thing was a great surprise to him. That, at least, was the way he told it later. Mark Twain was never one to let a few facts get in the way of a good story. He had known in the summer that the Century Company was planning a series of articles on the Civil War by participants, and ultimately a book. As a budding publisher, he was looking for good manuscripts. He at once conceived the idea of getting Century's book away from them. From his summer home in Elmira he wrote to Webster that "We want the Century's warbook — keep on the best of terms with those folks." Perhaps he had not known that Grant was writing for *Century* and planning to go on with a book of his own, though the essential story had appeared in Baltimore and New York newspapers. There is no record that he went to Long Branch that summer, and he had been out of the city later. Webster may not have followed up, or he may himself have been out of touch with his partner.[36]

Twain went to see Grant the very next morning, if his memory served him properly, to see how far the book idea had developed and what the plans for publication were. A letter from Webster to Twain, November 28, 1884, indicates that the visit was more formal: "Col. Fred Grant writes that he will see you on the subject of his father's new book at any time," Webster told him. The general had gone to the Century Company office on October 22, the same day, probably by sheer coincidence, that he visited a doctor on another matter. "General Grant has just been in," Gilder recorded, "spent some time and wants us to publish his book or books." The general by this time was evidently thinking in terms of more than one volume. The publishers had leisurely prepared a draft contract and, when Twain called on the Grants at the end of November, it was under discussion by the general and his son.[37]

They allowed Twain to look over the proposed terms. Grant said that there was no objection whatever to his seeing the contract, since it had proceeded no further than a mere consideration of its details, without promise given or received on either side. He supposed that the offer was fair and right, and he had been expecting to accept it and conclude the bargain. He read it aloud to his visitor. "I didn't know whether to cry or laugh," Mark recorded not long after. The Century people were offering only the customary 10 percent royalty for a book that was bound to sell several hundred thousand copies in the first year of publication, the same royalty "which they would have offered to any unknown Comanche Indian whose book they had reason to believe might sell 3,000 or 4,000 copies." He told Grant that the offer was absurd and should not be considered for an instant. The royalty should be doubled. Grant should consult another publisher. Mark was publishing his own next book, he said, and would soon have the best-equipped subscription house in the country. The general demurred, saying that the book should go to the man who had first suggested it to him. "General, if that is so, it belongs to *me*," Twain took him up. Grant did not understand until Twain reminded him that he had long ago urged the general to write his memoirs. Fred Grant now joined in, urging that the matter be delayed until the publishing possibilities could be more carefully inquired into.[38]

Twain then went on another lecture tour, leaving the matter in the hands of his partner Webster and Colonel Grant. "I wanted the General's book, and I wanted it very much," he said later, "but I had very little expectation of getting it." He thought that the Century Company would meet the higher terms without question. The general called on his old Philadelphia and Long Branch friend Childs for advice. Childs found that it was plain that Grant wanted to give the book to Twain, if only on the score of friendship. By this time the success of *Huckleberry Finn* was fairly certain, and Twain's firm seemed as capable as any to publish the memoirs. After investigation, with the help of lawyers, Childs and Colonel Fred agreed that Charles L. Webster & Co. should have the book. Arrangements were made for drawing the contract. This time, at least, Webster kept his partner advised of what was going on. "It would be a grand thing if we could get the General's book on those terms," Twain wrote him from Indianapolis on February 8. "Dear Uncle Sam," Webster replied a few days later, "I have been working like a beaver and I have at last got that Grant matter in first rate train as you will see by the enclosed correspondence. . . . There's big money for us both in that book and on the terms indicated in my note to the General we can make it pay *big."* The publication was a good bit of an undertaking, he said, but he hoped they would get the book, "and that seems a certainty now." [39]

Webster's final offer had been either a 20 percent gross royalty or 70 percent of the net profits. Grant was afraid that Mark was in danger of bankrupting himself out of pure friendship. He felt that he was taking unfair advantage. He wrote to Twain asking him which of the two propositions would be best all around. Twain said that the 20 percent royalty would be best. Grant then decided to take the other. That way, if the book should be a failure, the publishers would not have to pay him anything. The contract also contained an appendix, transferring the book to Mrs. Grant, and from her to Webster & Co., for the consideration of $1,000 cash. This was to prevent the general's creditors from seizing the proceeds of the book. [40]

The Century Company were naturally very much chagrined at losing the book. When the news became public that Charles L. Webster & Co., instead of Century, was going to publish Grant's memoirs, the New York *World* thought that there had been a real "falling out" between Grant and Century.

It was doubted that any more of Grant's articles would appear in the magazine, even though they had been advertised. "The *Century* people said they had no grievance, but are reported to be exceedingly 'sore' about the matter." Johnson insisted later that they would have bettered their terms if they had known what Mark Twain's firm was offering, but that they did not. "The General," he wrote acidly, "who knew nothing of the customs or etiquette of the publishing business, had been won over by the humorist." It is scarcely credible that the Century Company did not know what was being offered, as the whole publishing world had become interested in the situation and Grant had many offers. It is clear that Century was outmaneuvered. Johnson, in his recollections, thought that Roswell Smith's neglect to clinch the deal earlier was a signal failure in an otherwise successful publishing career. As Mark Twain remembered it, Smith, "with the glad air of a man who has stuck a nail in his foot," congratulated him on getting the book. He told Twain that Grant had wanted him to insure a sale of twenty-five thousand sets of the book, and that "I wouldn't risk such a guaranty on any book that was ever published." [41] Smith seems to have been a little lacking in imagination, to say the least. But there was natural caution in his attitude, as Twain himself discovered.

When Mark returned to New York from his tour he called on Grant. The date was February 21, 1885. Grant told him definitely that he was to have the book. Twain was astonished to see how thin and weak the general looked. He was astonished because, while there had been sensational reports that Grant was suffering from cancer, these had just been denied. The *World,* quoting a professional medical journal, had only the day before said that "all the more serious and alarming symptoms" of Grant's illness had virtually disappeared. The illness, thought to have been cancerous, "would appear to have been a case of chronic superficial inflammation of the tongue," probably caused by excessive smoking. "I took for granted the report," Twain recorded a few days later, "and said I had been glad to see that news. He smiled and said, 'yes—if it had only been true.' " One of Grant's physicians was present and told Twain that the general's condition was anything but encouraging. [42]

2. The General Is Stricken

GENERAL GRANT had been in excellent health. A letter from Long Branch to the *Denver News* in the summer of 1882 described his modest cottage there, in the midst of ostentation. "The short, stumpy figure of the ex-President" was as familiar at Long Branch as it had been in Washington, and in his drives and walks he was continually tipping his hat to acknowledge salutations. "He has a house full," the reporter said, "and a happy family of children and grandchildren about him now, and in his ruddy prime Gen. Grant very freely says that he is quite as comfortably fixed as he wants to be." But on Christmas Eve, 1883, he slipped on the icy sidewalk as he was reaching up to give a bill as a Christmas present to his coachman and fell heavily, striking his left leg against the edge of the curbstone. It was thought to be only a bruise and a shock to the sciatic nerve, but he was laid up for weeks and continued to be somewhat lame thereafter. The terrible blow of business failure a few months later probably affected his health adversely. His lameness ceased to mend and his strength to return.[1] He was still on crutches when he attended the reunion of the Army of the Potomac society the following June, and was seldom without a cane to the end. The leg had been injured twice before in falls from horses—once during a military review at New Orleans, and again a few weeks later when Grant was crossing the mountains to beleaguered Chattanooga.

In the early summer of 1884, as Mrs. Grant told the story years afterward, "while they were all at dinner one day, General Grant took a peach and began to eat it; suddenly he rose from the table and began pacing the floor, complaining that the peach had hurt his throat. He seemed to be suffering acutely." Later he told his neighbor, Mr. Childs, that he had a troublesome dryness in his throat and suffered pain whenever he ate a peach. Childs told him that Dr. Da Costa, one of the most eminent physicians in the country, was coming from Philadelphia for a visit, and said he would have the doctor look at Grant's throat. When Da Costa arrived he went over to the general's cottage, gave him a careful examination, wrote a prescription, and asked who Grant's family physician was. The general said it was Dr. Fordyce Barker. Da Costa advised him to see Barker at once.[2]

But Dr. Barker was in Europe, and Grant, though evidently suffering pain, was now engrossed in his writing. He asked Childs several times if he had seen Da Costa, and talked of going to Philadelphia for a few days with Childs and have a talk with him, but took no action. Barker was not expected back from Europe until October, and Grant evidently felt that he should observe the proprieties and consult with him before going to a specialist. After Grant had moved back to New York and Barker had come home, he was referred to Dr. John H. Douglas, the leading throat specialist of the city.[3] By this time the disease had a start of several months.

On October 22 the general came to Dr. Douglas's office, bringing a card from Dr. Barker. Douglas had served with the U. S. Sanitary Commission during the Civil War. He had met Grant shortly after the battle of Fort Donelson, and had developed a great admiration for him. He now asked the general what he could do for him, and Grant said that he had difficulty in swallowing. After a local examination, in which the doctor found the soft palate inflamed, dark, and scaly, "strongly suggestive of epithelial trouble," and the tongue somewhat rigid at the base on the right side, Grant asked him, "is it cancer?" Douglas told him, in effect, but without using the dreaded word itself, that it probably was: "General, the disease is serious, epithelial in character, and sometimes capable of being cured." Badeau had moved into the Grant house by this time. He said that when the general returned from his visit to Douglas, he seemed serious but not alarmed. The physician "had told him that his throat was affected by a complaint with a cancerous tendency." [4]

Grant came to Douglas again the next day, with his faithful colored valet Harrison Tyrrell, and Mrs. Grant came with her son Fred a few days later. Douglas took measures for lessening the congestion, for prophylaxis, and for removing odors from ulcerated surfaces, and instructed the family in how they could help. He warned them particularly against irritating applications. He told them that the disease would take a long course, with varying stages of depression and hope. The Grants, Douglas recorded, carried out his injunctions strictly and devotedly. During the next two months the congestion diminished, while the general, though visiting Douglas almost daily, continued hard at work on his memoirs. There were occasional low periods, however. Late in December, General Edward F. Beale, a Washington friend, reported to the newspapers that he had had a letter from Grant in which he said that he was in very poor health, and a later one from Fred Grant in which he stated that his father was confined to his room and that his condition was such as to alarm the family. Beale didn't know what the trouble was, but thought that it was the result of anxiety over financial problems.[5]

Early in January rumors spread that Grant was suffering from cancer of the tongue, and the *New York Times* sought to track them down. Interviews with Dr. Barker and Dr. Douglas gave some foundation for a cheerful story. The pain which had given rise to the rumors had been greatly relieved, Barker said. "The General is cheerful and comfortable, and spends a great part of his time at home writing the history of his military life, which is to be published by a prominent house as soon as it is completed." Barker said that the general's health had improved very much during the last few weeks, and he gave some details. Among other things, he and Douglas had persuaded Grant to give up cigar smoking. "The improvement in his condition since then is marvelous." Extraction of a bad tooth had also helped. Douglas was more reticent, and at first refused to discuss the case at all. But when the report of cancer of the tongue was mentioned, he said: "Gen. Grant has not cancer of the tongue. The difficulty is in his mouth, and it is of an epithelial character. The irritation has now been greatly relieved, and that is all I feel at liberty to say." Out of this information, definitely guarded though it was on Douglas's part, the *Times* built a headline saying, "Gen. Grant in Better Health." Grant wrote a letter to his sister, in Switzerland just at this time, telling her that "My mouth has been very sore, but not so bad, I think, as some of the newspapers have made out." He was busy on his book, he said, "which Fred is copying for the press." He hoped to have it ready by May.[6]

The story popped up again early in February, when the New York *World* announced, "Gen. Grant Very Ill." It quoted a Philadelphia source as stating "that Gen. Grant has been obliged to decline Mr. George W. Child's invitation to visit him on account of ill-health." It was said that he was troubled with soreness at the root of the tongue, which caused him great pain when he attempted to swallow. "He has not smoked since Nov. 20." Grant made his last call on Dr. Douglas on February 16. On this visit he caught cold. After that Douglas treated him at his home, and Dr. Barker also made regular calls. The small ulcers present in the throat now became active, and there were other alarming symptoms. A formal consultation was held in the light of what would today be called a biopsy. Dr. George B. Elliott, an expert microscopist, was given a piece of tissue from Grant's throat and pronounced it cancerous. Douglas and Barker called in Drs. H. B. Sands and T. M. Markoe, and on February 19 a thorough examination was made. The method of treatment already employed was approved; the practicability of an opertion to remove the diseased tissue was considered and abandoned. "The conclusion was reached that the disease was an epithelioma, or epithelial cancer of the malignant type, that was sure to end fatally." [7]

The medical men withheld the news for some time, and meanwhile a very cheerful story on Grant's condition, based on earlier information, appeared in the *World*. At the end of the month the *World* reversed itself. A story from Philadelphia, based on reliable medical authority from New York, said: "Not withstanding the rose-colored report of Gen. Grant's health, recently given in a medical journal, the truth is that Gen. Grant is a very sick man, and his death apparently not far distant." The condition of his mouth and tongue gave evidence of a malignant and fatal disease, his injured hip was still painful, and he was also suffering terribly from neuralgia. In the midst of his sufferings, "He works every day with bandaged head and an unremitting pain to finish his military autobiography or history of the war and hopes to complete it this spring." The doctors could no longer withhold the facts and on March 1 the *New York Times* announced that the general was "Sinking Into the Grave," that "Gen. Grant's Friends Give Up Hope," and that he was "Dying Slowly From Cancer." A consultation had been held on February 19, it was revealed, "at which it was agreed that the trouble from which the General was suffering was cancer, and the only difference of opinion was as to the probable rapidity of its development." If the disease were in any other part of the body, Dr. Douglas said, it could be held in abeyance, but "The consulting physicians had all agreed that no operation would be of use." [8]

Mark Twain's visit to the general on February 21 had, therefore, been made when a very optimistic story about Grant had just appeared, but shortly after what amounted to a sentence of death had been pronounced. Twain, trying to cover his shock at Grant's appearance and the discouraging tone of Dr. Douglas's remarks, had said that the general's trouble was probably due to smoking, and that it was a warning to those who smoked to excess, himself included. Douglas, whose sterling virtues seem not to have included a sense of humor, thought that this was not the sole nor even the major cause; that depression and distress of mind resulting from Grant's financial disaster was a more important factor. When Twain was ready to go, Colonel Fred Grant went downstairs with him and stunned him by telling him confidentially that the physicians feared the general might not live more than a few weeks. The fact that the book contract was signed a few days later speaks much for Twain's courage. The memoirs were far from finished.[9]

Grant had been laboring faithfully at his literary tasks throughout his illness, the *World* noted. One of these was the series of articles for the *Century Magazine,* and the other his

John Hancock Douglas, M.D., the leading throat specialist in New York City. He had served with the U. S. Sanitary Commission during the Civil War. He had met Grant shortly after the battle of Fort Donelson and greatly admired him. Grant visited his office on October 22, 1884, and learned, in effect, that he suffered from throat cancer. — Courtesy of Mrs. Lee Gwynne Martin

"History of the Rebellion," in two volumes. He had been aware of the necessity of hurrying, "and in his desire to see it completed he frequently overtasked himself and thus aggravated his disease and hastened the end." His book was now practically completed, being so far advanced that even if the General should be unable to do any more work upon it, "it can be easily

George Frederick Shrady, M.D. Dr. Shrady was first called upon to help treat Grant early in 1885 and continued, along with Dr. Douglas, until the general's death in July of that year. This illustration is from Century Magazine, *May 1908.—Courtesy of General Research and Humanities Division; The New York Public Library; Astor, Lenox and Tilden Foundations*

finished by his son." The magazine articles on Shiloh, Vicksburg, Chattanooga, and the Wilderness were also completed. The first had already appeared. "The General recently revised the articles, and Mr. Johnson, of the *Century,* said yesterday that all the manuscript complete is now in his possession." [10] This story, as it developed, was highly overoptimistic. There was a great deal of work still to be done on the book, and there was a marked difference of opinion among the publishers about the completion of the *Century* articles.

Into the depression that filled the Grant household in these days there came one cheering note. There had been several attempts among the general's friends to pass a bill placing him on the army retired list as a full general. Now the bill was revived. Joseph E. Johnston, ex-Confederate general then in Congress, had undertaken to introduce the measure, but there was considerable opposition. Childs, who had undoubtedly been working for the bill, was visiting Grant on March 4, the last day of the session. Grant needed the income, of course, though Twain had already supplied him with an advance of $10,000 on his book, but the recognition of his services that the act would involve seems to have been uppermost in his mind. Childs tried to assure him that it would pass, but Grant said that it couldn't be done in the confusion of the last day of a session, and that he had given up all expectation. While he was talking to Grant, Childs received a telegram saying that the bill had passed. Grant seemed quietly gratified, but Mrs. Grant was jubilant. When she came in and Childs told her the news, she cried out, "Hurrah! our old commander is back!" Mark Twain was there, too, and later also stressed Grant's iron control of the emotion that he must have felt. But a telegram that he sent to Mrs. Clemens the same day said that he was present when the telegram was put in Grant's hands, and that "The effect upon him was like raising the dead." [11]

The publication of Grant's book on the scale that Twain visualized was an enormous undertaking. He quickly canceled a projected reading trip to England and Australia. He wanted, he said, to be "close at hand all the time while General Grant's book is passing through the press & being canvassed. I want no mistakes to happen, nothing overlooked, nothing neglected." Webster, in technical charge, became furiously busy, while Mark rushed back and forth between Hartford and New York, between the publishing office on 14th Street and the Grant home on 66th Street, boiling with ideas and issuing a constant stream of orders, suggestions, and admonitions. Estimates and prices for vast quantities of paper were considered, all available presses were contracted for, and binderies were pledged exclusively for the Grant book. Applications for subscription agencies poured in. Webster called a meeting of the heads of such agencies. "By the time these men returned to their homes," Twain's biographer says, "they had practically pledged themselves to a quarter of a million sets of the *Grant Memoirs,* and this estimate they believed to be conservative." [12]

The subscription publication of *Huckleberry Finn* was turning out well. "This result sets my fears at rest as regards the General's book," Twain wrote Webster from Hartford at the middle of March. "It *insures* a sudden sale of 250,000 copies of the first volume." But even the first volume was not complete, he had found. "As I understand it, it lacks 2 or 3 chapters. Well, if the lack is at the *end* of the volume, we will end the volume *without* them; if they are to be supplied by another hand, they may begin the 2d vol., not mar the 1st, which must be *all* General Grant, if possible." [13] Mark's profits from *Huckleberry Finn,* and all the other cash he could lay his hands on, were to be tied up in the publication of Grant's *Personal Memoirs* for many months. It was an exciting but risky venture, in the light of the general's physical condition, and he had to face the likelihood that Grant would not live to complete the book.

Dr. George F. Shrady, an eminent physician and editor of the New York *Medical Record,* who had confirmed Dr. Elliott's microscopic analysis of Grant's throat tissue sample without knowing whose it was, was called into consultation early in March. Another gathering of doctors and another detailed examination confirmed the earlier diagnosis. With Barker and Douglas, Dr. Henry B. Sands, "the famous surgeon," and Dr.

Shrady "made a very formal and careful examination of the throat of the patient, using for the purpose the ordinary circular reflecting-mirror fastened on the forehead by a band around the observer's head." The disease had obviously made progress, the local malady having increased and the adjacent parts having become more infiltrated. The advisability of an operation on the general was again discussed and rejected. "The wisdom of such a decision," according to Dr. Shrady, "was manifested in sparing him unnecessary mutilation and allowing him to pass the remainder of his days in comparative comfort. Relatively, however, it meant suffering for him until the end." [14]

Grant had evidently been revising his first volume and was still writing when, on March 20, Mark Twain called on him, bringing along Karl Gerhardt, an amateur sculptor of Hartford, whom he had subsidized for extensive study in Paris. Gerhardt had made a bust of Twain, which was used as a frontispiece for *The Adventures of Huckleberry Finn*. He had also made a small clay bust of Grant from a photograph, and Twain had him bring it to New York to show to the Grant family. The Grant ladies became excited over it and insisted on taking Gerhardt into the general's room to have a look at his subject. They all walked around the old hero twittering and moving his head to new angles while he submitted serenely. "One marked feature of General Grant's character is his exceeding gentleness, goodness, sweetness," Mark recorded that night in his notebook. "I wonder it has not been more spoken of." Presently the general told Gerhardt to bring in his clay and work there. The ladies left; Gerhardt went to work at a small table set up for him; Twain picked up a book; and the general relaxed in his reclining chair and took a nap. After an hour or so, General Badeau came in with some sheets of manuscript in his hand, interrupting the general's nap. "I've been reading what you wrote this morning, General," he said, "and it is of the utmost value; it solves a riddle that has puzzled men's brains all these years and makes the thing clear and rational." Mark misunderstood the strategic point involved when he recorded the episode that night, but the little incident did illustrate what seems to have been the normal procedure; Grant was doing the writing and Badeau was adding his comments. Gerhardt's little bust of Grant was later widely reproduced in terra-cotta, and was regarded by many as the most nearly correct likeness of the general.[15]

The general had stopped the work of revising that day, the *New York Tribune* reported, "and wrote many pages of new material. He has gone back to his work with surprising zeal, and if there are no unfavorable developments he will continue writing and revising until the second volume is completed." But there were unfavorable developments soon after, and it seemed for weeks that Grant would do no more. His daughter Nellie Sartoris came home from England just at this time, and the excitement of meeting her, Dr. Douglas told reporters, on top of the fatigue of pushing on his literary work, resulted in insomnia. General Horace Porter, one of Grant's staff in the Virginia campaign, called a few days later, and told reporters that the general was weak and wasting away, but standing it all without a murmur. "To see him wasting and sinking in this way is more touching and excites deeper sympathy among his friends than if he made some sign of his suffering, as ordinary men do, by grumbling and complaining." On March 26 Grant did not feel equal to going on with his book, but took a short ride in the park with Dr. Douglas and his good friend Senor Romero. That evening he submitted to examination and cross-examination as a witness in the case of James D. Fish, then on trial for embezzlement. He seemed under no strain at the time, but had a sleepless night and Dr. Douglas thought the examination by the lawyers was to blame.[16]

Douglas had used a cocaine solution almost from the first, in local applications to reduce pain. As the disease progressed, morphine injections were increasingly needed to permit the general to sleep. Douglas left the house toward midnight on March 28, having given Grant the usual anodyne, but was hastily called back a few hours later. The general had wakened with a terrible fit of choking and coughing, from accumulations in his throat. Douglas and Shrady, who came in shortly, were able by heroic measures to help him clear his throat and the crisis passed. Several more violent coughing spells succeeded in the next few days, each one leaving him weaker, and more than once his life was despaired of. In one of these crises, Dr. Shrady used brandy injections as a stimulant. The Reverend Dr. John P. Newman, a fashionable Methodist minister, was spending a good bit of time at the Grant home. He had been the pastor of the Metropolitan Church in Washington during Grant's administration, and the president had attended services there. Mrs. Grant admired Newman greatly, and had asked him to come. Newman did much praying, and sought earnestly to interest the general in the state of his soul. He even baptized Grant during the worst of his sinking spells. The Grant ladies urged him to it, and Colonel Grant thought that "It would do no harm." While Newman was praying, Shrady was administering brandy by injection. There was a sudden turn for the better, and Newman of course attributed it to prayer. "With a similar gratification in the physical responsiveness of the patient," Shrady recorded later, "I was inclined to attribute the result to the brandy." It was "a very ordinary method of treatment in such cases," he said.[17]

After the desperate nature of Grant's illness had been confirmed, his house on East 66th Street, just off Fifth Avenue, became a focus of attention. The press, as the crisis deepened, spared no effort to obtain information. After a period of private life, Grant was again a figure of absorbing interest. Dr. Shrady was now fully committed to the case, and he and Dr. Douglas held regular consultations and issued formal bulletins. They knew that much contradictory information had been issued in the comparatively recent case of President Garfield, and they sought to state exact facts, within the sanction of the family. For some time there were always three bulletin boys in the main hall of the house, representing Western Union, the Associated Press, and the United Press. There was a general clearinghouse for news in the basement of a nearby house on Madison Avenue, and there the reporters gathered. All the metropolitan newspapers had special telegraph wires to their downtown offices, and reporters patrolled the street in front of Grant's house. One even made love to a chambermaid across the street to get a good window. Reporters remained on guard in relays in all weather. Any unusual light in the house brought them together. Visitors flocked to the house and could not always be turned away. Visitors and members of the household, leaving the house, were of course pounced upon by the press.[18]

One of Grant's violent coughing spells finally brought on a severe hemorrhage. Douglas, unable to determine its source, sent for Shrady and Sands. The hemorrhage ceased of its own accord, however, and an injection of morphine brought sleep. Almost at once, the general began to improve. "What charm had worked this change in the dying man no one knew," the *World* said. "The doctors said that the morphia and the stimulants were keeping life in him, but that these two factors should cool the fevered pulse of the general, make his respiration almost normal, and render him stronger they could not understand." By the middle of April he was reading the newspapers and even attempted briefly a little writing. He astonished the family one day by joining them for lunch, and ate some macaroni and cold mutton. Ex-Senator Chaffee, a heavy loser in the failure of Grant & Ward, was often at the house. He now gave out that the doctors' diagnosis might have been wrong; that Grant, in his opinion, did not have cancer at all but had been suffering from an ulcerated sore throat. He had no doubt that the general would pull through. "The people rejoice," the *World* commented with more than a touch of sarcasm, "that their great soldier Grant, whose death a syndicate of doctors led them to expect at any moment for the past five weeks, is now apparently on the high road to recovery." Shrady, asked about this, assured reporters that there had been no mistake. There was no reason to question the diagnosis. The disease was one of ups and downs, with a definite downward tendency.[19]

Grant now began driving out again into Central Park with Dr. Douglas or members of the family on pleasant days. On April 27, his birthday, he received a number of friends and later joined the family at dinner. The press guard had meanwhile relaxed and Grant's name almost disappeared from the front page for some time. The disease was still there, however, and the re-

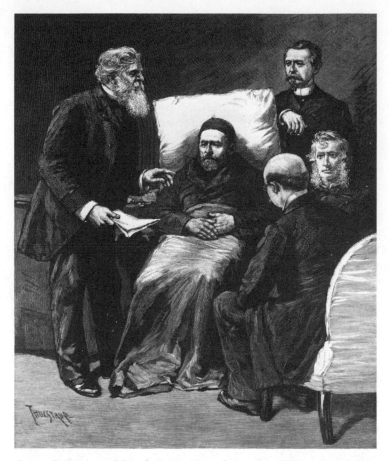

General Grant and his doctors. By early spring, 1885, several doctors were involved in the Grant case. Left to right in this illustration taken from Harper's Weekly, *April 18, 1885, are Dr. Douglas (standing), General Grant (seated, with blanket), Dr. Shrady (standing, with arm on chair), Dr. Sands (seated, facing Grant), and Dr. Barker (seated, facing front).—Courtesy of The New-York Historical Society, New York City*

covery was only temporary. It was, very likely, partly an effort of will. The general had ceased writing almost entirely for some weeks. Badeau had given up his room as the house had filled with relatives, but he still spent his days there. He was at the house all during the period of crisis, and seems to have made himself useful in various ways. Grant's papers were still in his study, Badeau recounted later, and "once in a great while he even yet attempted to write a page." Occasionally Badeau took down an idea from Grant's lips and read it back to him. But these efforts became rarer; "he had no longer strength for the effort, no longer interest in his work, and at last abandoned all idea of being able to finish it." [20]

If this was true, it was only a temporary weakness of spirit. Galley proofs of the first volume of Grant's *Memoirs* were now coming out and Mark Twain was reading them. This was something he probably never did for any other man. He told Webster that his marks could be transferred to the copy regularly sent to Colonel Grant: "My marks will not be seriously important, since they will concern grammar & punctuation only." Colonel Grant suggested to him that a little encouragement might help his father. Mark obliged handsomely by comparing some of Grant's chapters with *Caesar's Commentaries,* in their "clarity of state-ment, directness, simplicity, manifest truthfulness, fairness and justice toward friend and foe alike, soldierly candor and frank-ness, and soldierly avoidance of flowery speech." The general was pleased. He began to plan taking up the work again, and Webster supplied him with a stenographer to save him the ef-fort of writing.[21]

Just as Grant was gathering his forces for a new effort, a story appeared in the New York *World* to the effect that he wasn't writing his own book at all. Its Washington correspondent had filled a column of "National Capital Gossip" with stories about Grant, chiefly if not entirely from General George P. Ihrie, who had known Grant well in the army. The anecdotes were highly complimentary, on the whole, but the columnist concluded: "Another false idea of Gen. Grant is given out by some of his friends, and that is that he is a writer. He is not a writer. He does not compose easily. Writing for him is a labor. The work upon his new book about which so much has been said is the work of Gen. Adam Badeau. Gen. Grant I have no doubt has furnished all of the material and all of the ideas in the memoirs as far as they have been prepared, but Badeau has done the work of composition. The most that Gen. Grant has done upon the book has been to prepare the rough notes and memoranda for its various chapters." Grant's greatness as a soldier should not be obscured by foolish misrepresentation. He was not a man who could chain himself down to a desk to write. He had always been a man of action. "He is so great that he can well afford to have the exact truth told about him." [22]

Grant read the newspapers regularly whenever he was able to, and he did not miss this story. The same day that it appeared, he spent considerable time looking over his unfinished manuscript "and expressed himself as feeling strong enough to take up the work where he left it more than a month ago." The next day he worked three hours on his book, "and for the first time employed a stenographer. He dictated clearly and succinctly for one hour without a break." The dictation, it was estimated, would cover about twenty-five pages of the book. Colonel Grant told reporters that evening that his father was dictating the Appomattox campaign, "and from his despatches and other data is enabled to give a perfectly straight and lucid account to the stenographer." Mark Twain had read the *World*'s story, and characteristically exploded in wrath. "The General's work this morning is rather damaging evidence against the World's intrepid lie. The libel suit ought to be instituted at once," he wrote Colonel Fred.[23]

But the general handled the matter in his own direct fashion. He wrote a letter to Charles L. Webster & Co., intended for the press. He quoted the pertinent statements in the *World*'s story about the book and commented on them briefly. "The composition," he said flatly, "is entirely my own." It was true, as stated, that he had furnished all of the material and all of the ideas for the memoirs; he had also "done the entire work of composition and preparing notes, and no one but myself has ever used one of

After he had been close to death, Grant's health seemed briefly to improve late in April 1885. This illustration showing the general leaving his house for a ride in the park appeared in Frank Leslie's Illustrated Newspaper, *May 2, 1885.—Courtesy of General Research and Humanities Division; The New York Public Library; Astor, Lenox and Tilden Foundations*

such notes in any composition." He pointed out that it was to the interest of the publisher to correct the false report, "which places me in the attitude of claiming the authorship of a book which I did not write, and it is also injurious to you who are publishing and advertising such book as my work." Twain's office immediately gave Grant's letter to the press, and it appeared in both the *New York Tribune* and the New York *Sun* a few days later. The *Tribune* used the subhead, "A Characteristic Answer to a False Statement": the *Sun,* no friend of Grant's, nevertheless observed editorially that the general's contradiction of the story was unnecessary. Grant had "the ability to write a peculiarly compact, distinct, picturesque, and telling English style." Badeau had a good deal more of ordinary literary culture than the general and was an experienced and able writer, but "the soldier is, in our judgment, in this case immensely superior to the journalist." [24]

It was strangely obtuse, therefore, of Badeau to write to Grant just at this time, demanding more money for his services and suggesting strongly that the general could not finish the book without him. Mark Twain knew by the beginning of May that orders for 60,000 sets of Grant's book had been received, and estimated that 300,000 would eventually be sold. No doubt he told the general at once. Anyway, Badeau knew of it when he wrote the general on May 2, presenting the letter in person and then walking out. He had also seen the new stenographer at work. His letter made it clear that he wanted a share in the profits now in prospect, and that he felt degraded by having, instead of dealing directly with Grant, to take copy from a stenographer and "piece and prepare and connect the disjointed fragments into a connected narrative." This was mere drudgery. He had no desire for the reputation or name of writing the book, he insisted: "The preposterous assertions in the newspapers will refute themselves." But the book was to have "a circulation of hundreds of thousands," while his own work on Grant's military career would be stamped out. The more he helped with the *Memoirs,* the more he was destroying his own reputation as Grant's historian. If he did not do it, his own book would retain its place, "for you have neither the physical strength nor the habits of mind yourself to make the researches to verify or correct your own memory. If you cannot yourself finish the work, nobody can do it fitly but me." For this work he wanted $1,000 a month, paid in advance, until the work was done, and afterward 10 percent of the entire profits.[25]

Grant's reply was devastating. His pride had been stung. The commercial success of his book was now assured, he had his pay as a retired general of the army, and money was no longer the prime objective. "The real trouble," Bruce Catton observes of this correspondence, which came to light only years later, "was that Grant had become a writing man, and he was driven by the writing man's compulsions." He had concluded, he wrote Badeau on May 5, "that you and I must give up all association as far as the preparation of any literary work goes which is to bear my signature." He hoped that otherwise their relations might continue, as they had always been, pleasant and friendly. He answered Badeau's long letter paragraph by paragraph. His book, he believed, would not supplant Badeau's, but rather enhance it. As to the drudgery of connecting disjointed fragments into a connected narrative, which Badeau found so distasteful, "I do not admit that disjointed nature of the matter you speak of, except of that part I wrote after I became so ill that I could write but little at a time." At that time, he admitted, "I supposed some one, whose name would necessarily be given to the public, and that name yours, would finish the book." Badeau had done little with the more than 100 pages of manuscript already in the hands of the stenographer. At this rate he would never finish the book. "To be frank, I do not believe the work would ever be done by you in case of my death while $1,000 per month was coming in." Besides, Badeau, whom he termed petulant, quarrelsome, and arrogant, would have become so arrogant that "there would have been a rupture between you and my family before many days had elapsed." As for Badeau's demand for 10 percent of the profits, it was preposterous. "This would make you a partner with my family as long as the book found a sale." As for the need of some literary man to supply his deficiencies,

that man being Badeau, "I do not want a book bearing my name
to go before the world which I did not write to such an extent as
to be fully entitled to the credit of authorship." He could not
think of holding himself "as dependent upon any person to supply a capacity which I am lacking. I may fail, but I will not put
myself in any such position." [26]

Badeau, who was suing the Grant family when these letters
were finally published in 1888, made Colonel Fred the villain in
the piece. The evidence is overwhelming that nearly everyone
who had long and intimate association with General Grant became devoted to him. It did not follow that they became devoted
to each other. Both Badeau and Colonel Grant had been helping the general with his literary work since the summer of 1884.
They had been cooped up together for many months under very
trying circumstances. Jealousy developed between them and
deepened into sheer hatred. Badeau insisted, when the colonel
finally gave the letters to the press, that he had never claimed to
have written Grant's book, but he had suggested much and made
many changes in the draft: "There was not a page in the first
volume nor one in the second, down to the Wilderness campaign, which did not contain a dozen alterations or modifica-
tions entirely my own." When the general's death had appeared
imminent, he charged, Colonel Grant approached him and asked
him to finish the book, allowing the colonel to put his name to
it. This Badeau refused. Later the general had asked them to
finish it together, but there was on Badeau's part "at no time any
desire to enter into collaboration with Colonel Grant." After the
story in the *World* appeared, stating that Badeau was writing the
book, both Colonel Grant and the publishers put pressure on
him to deny that he had written a line of it. He refused, and
"had high words on the subject with Colonel Grant." He had
finally agreed to sign a brief letter to the general, stating that he
disclaimed authorship and that "What assistance I have been
able to render has been in suggestion, revision or verification."
Grant's crushing letter dated the next day, Badeau claimed, was
really Colonel Fred's work. If the general had not been
"drugged, diseased and under the influence of his son," he

would not have put his name to "a paper unworthy of his fame." [27]

All this is very distressing, of course, and some of it unquestionably the product of Badeau's embittered imagination. Colonel Grant was able, when the whole affair was finally aired, to show reporters the original draft of his father's letter of May 5, 1885, in the general's well-known hand. "That is the letter Badeau gives me the credit of writing," he told them, "and after he says I was too big a fool to write a word for my father's book. I wish I could write such a letter." But Badeau did have a grievance. The general had given him a written agreement to pay him $5,000 out of the first $20,000 profits from the book, and $5,000 more out of the next $10,000. Badeau had received only $250, which was one-quarter of the $1,000 "earnest money" that the publishers had paid the general on the signing of the contract. Later the Grant family refused for years to pay him the rest. On May 9, Badeau acknowledged Grant's letter and said that he would "make no attempt to change your views." Grant, he said, looked upon his assistance "as that of an ordinary clerk or literary hack; I thought I was aiding you as no one else could in doing a great work." He had not changed his feelings and intended to write another book about the general. Meanwhile, "As the occasion for remaining at your house is at an end, I will send for my trunks and boxes as soon as I have secured lodgings, and pay my respects to yourself and family when I return to town." He and Grant never met again.[28]

In early May Dr. Barker left again for Europe. The general thanked him for his long professional friendship, and added: "I suppose you never expect to see me again." "I hope I may," Barker replied. Grant answered a little sadly, "You do not say 'expect' but 'hope.' " The general had worked prodigiously at the beginning of the month, in the midst of the controversy with Badeau. "In two days General Grant has dictated 50 pages of foolscap," Mark Twain wrote exultantly to his friend Howells, "& thus the Wilderness & Appomattox stand for all time in his own words. This makes the second volume of his book as valuable as the first. He looks mighty well these latter days." But sometimes the general's voice failed him and he had to give up dictation and return to writing. For days at a time he could do no work at all. Doggedly he returned to it whenever he was able. In the middle of the month, with the weather turning warm, the cancer became active again and for a time a new crisis was feared. Dr. Douglas had some time before let it be known that his patient was to be moved to the mountains for the summer and now thought that, if the weather continued warm, the sooner he was moved the better. "The air up where he is going is delicious and will do him good." [29]

Within a day or two, however, the usual semiweekly conference between Douglas and Shrady resulted in a report that there was no marked downward change. Swelling behind Grant's ear, which had become noticeable, had subsided and there was less pain. The general, whose voice had become somewhat husky, "dictated for several hours to the stenographer" and later began compiling notes for future dictation. In general, he seemed much improved. On May 23 the *New York Tribune* reported that "The story of the General's campaigns is about finished." His labor would now "be confined to revising his manuscript, every word being carefully considered before it is sent to the publisher." Three days later Mark Twain, who always came on call to cheer and comfort the general, talked with him about his first campaign in Missouri in 1861, when Mark and his amateur Confederate comrades had run at the mere rumor that Grant was approaching. "It is curious and dreadful," he recorded, "to sit up in this way and talk cheerful nonsense to General Grant, and he under sentence of death with that cancer. He says he has made the book too large by 200 pages—not a bad fault. A short time ago we were afraid we would lack 400 of being enough." [30]

At the beginning of June, Dr. Douglas gave out a cheerful account of his patient's condition. Swelling had subsided, and the general had been eating solid foods in very moderate quantity. "Dr. Douglas expects Gen. Grant will have left the city before the last week of this month," the *Times* reported. Colonel Grant said that his father was suffering less pain and seemed brighter. "His book is now entirely off his mind, and what he now does is more amusement than otherwise for father." He did not fear any reaction after the completion of the work, he said, but unquestionably, marked by periods of a week at a time, there was a loss of strength and vigor, and the general was certainly growing thinner.[31]

Both Colonel Grant and Mark Twain evidently believed that the book really was finished. On June 8 Charles L. Webster & Co. issued a prospectus of Grant's *Personal Memoirs* to the subscription canvassers across the country and overseas. It was intended to issue the first volume on December 1 and the second volume the following March. Extensive quotations in the prospectus covered material from Grant's early years to Appomattox. Evidently there was a completed draft, a great part of which had already been set in type. But the general, it soon became apparent, was far from satisfied with his work. Mark Twain's firm had enlarged the book to contain the excess copy already written, but they found that Grant was still going to stick in, here and there, "no end of little plums and spices." [32]

3. Mount McGregor Becomes a Summer Resort

THE MEDICINAL virtues of springs in the general vicinity of Saratoga were known to the Indians. The Mohawks in 1767 took their ailing friend Sir William Johnson to one of these springs to drink the waters. He was greatly benefited. The word of what seemed a remarkable cure to one of the most distinguished men in the American colonies spread quickly. Visitors began to journey to the springs even before the Revolution.[1] The long years of the struggle for independence, in which the Mohawks took the British side and the whole New York frontier was a scene of recurring devastation and slaughter, interrupted the traffic. It began again with the coming of peace, and by the early nineteenth century Ballston Spa was a popular health resort, with summer hotels and boarding houses. Its mineral springs had a worldwide reputation. Saratoga Springs, a few miles to the north, became its rival beginning in 1802, when Gideon Putnam built there the first Grand Union Hotel.[2] Saratoga Springs eventually eclipsed its competitor, and by the middle of the century was a center of wealth and fashion. An authoritative travel guide described it in 1857 as "the most famous place of summer resort in the United States," with ten hotels and numerous boarding houses. In or near the village were twelve medicinal springs, the most famous being the Congress Spring, whose waters were bottled and sent all over the world.[3] Saratoga Springs rose to further heights of fashion and popularity after the Civil War.

The rugged region of the Adirondack Mountains to the north began to be exploited for its timber during the same period. While the lumber rush was still far from its peak, another use of this wild and beautiful country developed. Gentlemen of means began organizing hunting and fishing trips to the Adirondacks, and the professional hunters and trappers who had moved in as the Indians left gradually developed a new specialty and became guides. Hunting camps, at first crude and temporary, came to be sometimes elaborate structures intended for use year after year. In 1858 the Saturday Club of Boston, a group of the intelligentsia that included Ralph Waldo Emerson and Louis Agassiz, spent part of a summer in the Adirondacks, attracting a good bit of attention.[4] The big rush to the Adirondacks began after the Civil War, with the publication in 1869 of the Reverend William Henry Harrison Murray's book, *Adventures in the Wilderness, or Camp Life in the Adirondacks.* This book, extolling the virtues of the outdoor life and the health-giving qualities of the Adirondacks in particular, became immensely popular and started a mass migration that took on the proportions of a gold rush. Summer hotels and permanent summer camps began to replace hunters' lodges, and railroads to support them pushed up into the mountains.[5]

Outlying spurs of the Adirondacks came within 10 miles of Saratoga Springs. The scenery immediately around the springs was dull and the air sometimes became oppressive, but a little to the north the abrupt Palmertown range offered a wilderness setting, cooler air, and spectacular views. The two attractions were brought into commercial contact by an enterprising gentleman from nearby Glens Falls, where the Hudson River tumbles out of the Adirondacks. Duncan McGregor, born in 1808 at the family homestead in Wilton, at the foot of the mountains, had been a farmer and later became a lumberman. He moved to the falls in 1867, and soon afterward his attention was drawn to the possibilities of a new activity. A visitor from South Carolina, it was recounted later, became enthusiastic over the attractions of the mountains so close to the fashionable resort of Saratoga. McGregor listened and, after careful inspection on his own, thought that one of the peaks of the Palmertown range could be developed into a popular mountain park.[6]

He began buying up parcels of land on the mountain, some at tax sales, until he acquired nearly a thousand acres including the summit and the eastern slope. The top of the mountain was already a popular local picnic spot, accessible only by trail. The mountain was named for him by the Reverend Robert G. Adams, the Methodist minister in Wilton, who had organized a town picnic on the summit in 1872. McGregor, at the time, was cutting a road up the mountainside; this road was at first the only route to the summit, and it is still in use a large part of the way. McGregor gradually extended his operations, opening a sawmill on a slope of the mountain and building a small hotel and other structures with lumber cut there. The little hotel, known as the Mountain House, at the highest point of the summit, was opened in the season of 1878. It was reported that "A few families have already discovered this charming resort the first year it has been opened, and are boarding steadily with Mr. McGregor." [7] McGregor's hotel and resort, gradually improved and expanded, prospered in a modest way, and a good many people drove out from Saratoga in the summer to enjoy the fresh air, the inspiring view of the Hudson Valley and neighboring mountains, the good country food, and the clean beds provided at modest prices. But McGregor was no longer young and he did not have the resources for large-scale development. A group of promoters saw big possibilities in the site and he sold out to them. In the summer of 1885, reporters on the mountain were told that it had taken a bait of $50,000 to tempt him off the mountain, and that he had cannily reserved for himself a place in the directorate of the new development company.[8]

W. J. Arkell of Canajoharie was the chief promoter. His father, James Arkell, was a substantial businessman and an influential Republican politician. Among other enterprises, the Arkells were in the meat-packing business and, in 1884, became proprietors, with Joseph W. Drexel of New York, of the *Albany Evening Journal*. W. J. Arkell was later a prominent figure in the field of periodical publication in New York City.[9] In his old age he recalled how he had come to take up the promotion of Mount McGregor. He and his father and brother had been at Saratoga Springs on the day of President Garfield's funeral in 1881. That afternoon they drove to Mount McGregor, "the handsomest spot, to my way of thinking, in America." John Kellogg of Amsterdam was of the party. "After we had enjoyed the beauties of the place," Arkell remembered, "he turned to me and asked: 'W. J., why don't you build a railroad to this beautiful spot?' 'How much will you contribute?' I asked him. 'Twenty-five thousand dollars,' he replied. My father said he would contribute $25,000, my brother came in with the same amount, and that left me to make it $100,000. That was a starter. In a very short time I raised $1,000,000 for the enterprise." [10]

Arkell and his associates first formed the Saratoga & Mt. McGregor Improvement Company, which appears to have been absorbed very soon into the Saratoga, Mount McGregor and Lake George Railroad Company. The first need in any major resort promotion on the mountain was for better and faster transportation to supplement the long, dusty carriage drive from Saratoga Springs. The railroad company moved fast. Chartered in February 1882, it broke ground in March and in July of the same year had cars running between the springs and the summit of the mountain. The line was built under the supervision of John McGee, who had long experience in building railroads in the Andes. The route from the northern edge of Saratoga Springs went for several miles in a fairly straight line northward, followed the foot of the mountains briefly, and then ascended the steep slope of Mount McGregor in a series of sharp curves. It was a narrow-gage road, but the ties were of trunk-line length and placed only 20 inches apart, so that the roadbed had the stability of a standard-gage line. The maximum grade was 212 feet to the mile, or approximately 4.1 percent. [11]

The railroad company seems to have had assurance that it would control the mountain, as well as its right of way, but did not complete the purchase of the land there from Duncan McGregor until the following February. Under existing New York law a railroad company could be formed and chartered by simply filing the necessary papers with the secretary of state. If it wanted to do other things than run a railroad, however, legislative authorization was necessary. A few weeks after the Saratoga, Mount McGregor and Lake George Railroad Company bought the mountain from McGregor, the legislature expanded its corporate powers considerably. It was authorized to purchase land "for pleasure parks and hotels, and to construct hotels and other buildings thereon, and use and operate the

The narrow-gage railroad depicted here, built in 1882, ran from Saratoga Springs to the summit of Mount McGregor. The ascent of the mountain involved a steep grade and a series of sharp curves. This illustration is taken from a small book of scenic views published in 1887.—Courtesy of the Historical Society of Saratoga Springs

same." [12] Arkell's group seems to have had considerable influence in Albany.

In the following season the company began building a large summer hotel, the Balmoral. The ideal spot for it, at the peak of the mountain and facing east, was already occupied by McGregor's little Mountain House. The summer dining room and kitchen were separate structures, and these were evidently demolished. The main building was carefully moved a few hundred feet down the slope to the southward and, in the fall of 1883, when work on the hotel was under way, became a boarding-house. [13]

Even before the hotel was finished, the mountain was embellished with an art gallery. In the summer of 1883 the Mount McGregor Art Association was not only in existence but also presenting a rather sophisticated exhibit there in an attractive little building, presumably built by and leased from the railroad company. Its catalogue, issued in that year, listed by title and painter 104 oils, 10 water colors, and 38 etchings. There were pictures by American artists popular at the time, some of whom are still remembered, and the prices were aimed at moneyed visitors. A. Bierstadt's *The Rocky Mountains* was hung there, priced at $1,500; Thomas Moran's *Hiawatha* was there, priced at $3,000; Arthur Quartley's *Summer Afternoon* was offered for $1,000. Water colorists exhibiting included W. T. Smedley and F. Hopkinson Smith, and there were etchings by J. M. Falconer, Stephen Parrish, and T. W. Wood. [14]

The hotel was completed in time for the season of 1884, and leased for three years by Cable, Bailey & Co. of New York. An illustrated advertising brochure issued in that year described its facilities and the other attractions of Mount McGregor in the glowing terms usually found in this type of publication. "A few years have made a marked change in the aspect of the summit of Mt. McGregor," the reader was informed, "without destroying the natural beauty of the landscape. A large, handsome and well-arranged summer hotel, under the capable management of Mr. Thomas Cable, now affords ample and pleasant accommodations for 300 boarders; and an elegant restaurant is open for transient visitors, who come merely to spend a few hours in this delightful resort." [15]

The hotel, which superseded the "modest though comfortable little hostelry erected by Mr. McGregor," had been constructed on the design of Messrs. Fuller, Wheeler & Prescott, architects and sanitary engineers of Albany. It was four stories in height, with piazzas 22 feet wide and 340 feet long, and balconies on the floors above. Each room commanded a pleasant view, those in front overlooking the Hudson Valley and those in the rear looking out "upon the green vistas of the primeval forest." The rooms were lighted by gas and the piazzas by electricity, "the Edison system." There was a 1,600-candlepower light on the top of the hotel. The building was arranged in the form of an obtuse triangle, so that its principal front and branching sides all faced generally toward the east. Ventilation for all rooms was as perfect as sanitary science could suggest, and the plumbing and drainage left nothing to be desired. It was claimed that on the hottest night of August, or rather "when it is hot everywhere else, the visitor at Hotel Balmoral will find a cool and refreshing air pervading the rooms and inviting to undisturbed repose." The cuisine, the reader was assured, was equal to the best in the United States. "For combined elegance and comfort," the brochure asserted confidently "the Balmoral is unsurpassed by any hotel in a country whose hotels are acknowledged to be the best in the world." [16]

Other attractions on Mount McGregor described in the brochure included "three beautiful sheets of water"—Lake Anna, Lake Bonita, and Artists' Lake. These had been left "in their own wild loveliness" without improvement except for a fleet of light cedar boats. The picture gallery, opened the year before, was described as "a beautiful structure, in the Queen Anne style of architecture." Some of the most popular artists of the country, it was noted, contributed their works to the gallery. The exhibitions would remain "a permanent and popular feature of the resort." The various views from the mountain top were extolled; rustic seats and arbors had been placed at selected points on the summit. To the east the view embraced the scene of the decisive campaign of the American Revolution, with the

This map is from a promotional piece entitled Mt. McGregor, the Popular Summer Sanitarium, Forty Minutes from Saratoga Springs (*Buffalo, 1884*).—*Courtesy of Local History and Genealogy Division; The New York Public Library; Astor, Lenox and Tilden Foundations*

Green Mountains beyond; southward the distant peaks of the Catskills could be seen; on the north were the rugged Adirondacks. An artesian well had been bored, providing an ample supply of pure water. The derrick, 90 feet high, had been left in position as an observatory from which the whole panorama could be viewed.[17]

The company, with a view to the needs of families that might wish to make the summit of Mount McGregor a summer and autumn home, and to enjoy more seclusion than a large hotel afforded, had "decided to permit the erection, under careful restrictions, of a limited number of handsome cottages, with a plot of ground to each one suited to the wishes of the purchaser." Title deeds to lots could be had at prices from $50 to $1,000; purchasers were forbidden to erect any cottage costing less than $1,500; and there were other restrictions "guarding imperatively against everything that could by any possibility detract from the peculiar charm of Mt. McGregor as a quiet and attractive Summer and Fall resort." It was pointed out that a lot and cottage on the mountaintop would be a very good investment, as well as a very desirable possession. Capitalists had found the erection of similar cottages at Saratoga Springs, Newport, Long Branch, and other summer resorts a very profitable source of income; from 20 to 30 percent a year was suggested as a likely return from cottages at Mount McGregor, with its longer season lasting well into October.[18]

In 1885 the leading local historian, who may easily have written the florid advertising brochure issued the year before, reviewed the history of the mountain in another booklet, asserting in conclusion that the summit of Mount McGregor, now so easily accessible, had "become one of the chief attractions of the great watering place" of Saratoga Springs. After quoting a line from William Howitt's *Book of the Seasons*, "Thanks be to God for the Mountains," he rhapsodized:

And the many thousands of summer tourists and pleasure-seekers who annually visit Saratoga, have not only the village itself, with its magnificent buildings rising with columned arch and castellated tower in fairy like proportions amid its shady streets, its verdant

lawns and bubbling fountains; they not only have Congress Spring
Park, which in its numerous attractions, combines the sweet repose
of nature with the fairest charms of art; not only Saratoga Lake, the
Race Course, and Judge Hilton's Woodlawn Park, already budding
into rare artistic beauty, to interest them, but they can also look
northward, and within easy morning ride climb the rugged brow of
Mount McGregor, and as they stand upon its summit they can view
the whole upper valley of the Hudson, teeming with its countless
historic memories; they can breathe there the pure invigorating air
fresh from the Great Wilderness, and while gazing upon them, they
too, with the sweet poet of Nature, can appreciatingly say, "Thanks
be to God for the mountains." [19]

It is highly unlikely that Joseph W. Drexel of New York City
was influenced by the lush promotional prose, but in the spring
of 1885 he bought the old McGregor hotel, which had been
moved from its original site to make way for the sumptuous
Hotel Balmoral. It was given out that he planned to renovate
the building and use it as a cottage part of the summer.[20] Drexel
was a member of the world-famous Philadelphia banking firm of
Drexel & Company. His older brother Anthony was the head
of the firm. Joseph had moved his base of operations to New
York after the Civil War, and had formed a partnership with
J. Pierpont Morgan. He was still president of the banking firm
of Drexel, Morgan & Company, and had other widespread banking connections, but he had ostensibly withdrawn from active
business in 1876 to devote his time to philanthropic, public, and
artistic enterprises. His interests were varied. Among other
activities, he served as treasurer of the New York Cancer
Hospital.[21]

Drexel already maintained a summer home in Saratoga
Springs, where he and his family came early in the season and
were leading figures in the life of the community. The cottage
on Mount McGregor, it was understood, was to be used merely
as a change from the social activity and occasional heat of the
village. The only other cottage on the mountain in 1885 was
that of W. J. Arkell, chief promoter of the resort. Arkell's cottage was the modified art gallery, which had evidently failed to
produce much revenue. Arkell had taken the building over,

moving it closer to the hotel, and he and his family occupied it during the summer.[22]

The Arkells and Drexel had only the year before taken over the *Albany Evening Journal*. The senior Arkell was a power in Republican politics and Drexel, it appears, was not without political ambitions himself. The *Journal* could be a powerful instrument toward any political objective. The ties between Drexel and the Arkells already extended beyond the newspaper business. When reporters from New York got aboard the narrow-gage train at the Saratoga Springs station on June 16, 1885, on their way to Mount McGregor, they noticed that the little locomotive was named *J. W. Drexel*.[23] On that same date an advertisement in the *New York Times* announced that the Hotel Balmoral, 1,200 feet above the sea, on Mount McGregor, near Saratoga, would open for the season on July 1. Actually, the hotel was already open, or about to open. The advertisement disappeared at once, but was replaced a few days later by one announcing that the Hotel Balmoral ("No Dew, No Malaria, No Mosquitoes, Certain Relief from Hay Fever") was "Now Open." [24] The season started unexpectedly early that year on Mount McGregor.

4. Last Days at Mount McGregor

THE COTTAGE that Joseph W. Drexel bought at Mount McGregor, ostensibly to afford him a change from the social activity and occasional sultry periods of the summer season in Saratoga, was destined and probably intended to serve a different purpose. With the approach of warm weather, there had been many suggestions on the advisability of a change of air for General Grant. There came offers from various country hotel proprietors, offering free room and board for the general and his family. It is hard to escape the thought that all of these offers were made with mixed motives. Grant's presence at any resort would go a long way to make its summer season successful. W. J. Arkell, promoter of Mount McGregor, recorded frankly in his old age that when General Grant was stricken with his fatal malady, "I thought if we could get him to come to Mount McGregor, and if he should die there, it might make the place a national shrine—and incidentally a success. So I went to Mr. Joseph W. Drexel, and through his efforts we got General Grant to come there." The story given to the press at the time, endlessly repeated and generally accepted, was a little different: Mr. Drexel had purchased the cottage for his own use; learning that Dr. Douglas was looking for some place "in the hills about Saratoga Springs," in which his distinguished patient might spend the summer, he immediately placed it at the general's disposal.[1]

There is no reason to impute mercenary motives to Drexel; he was a very wealthy man for the time, he was a real philanthropist, and he was a friend of Grant's. They had probably met more than once at Long Branch, where Drexel's brother Anthony, a business associate of Childs's, had a cottage near Grant's. They had known each other in the financial world of New York. When Grant was starting a subscription to the Statue of Liberty pedestal fund, Drexel had been one of only two others who signed it. Drexel, as treasurer of the New York Cancer Hospital, probably had a sympathetic interest in Grant's case.[2] Arkell was of another type, or at least at an earlier stage of his career. Money was important to him, and he was eager to make Mount McGregor pay off. It was reported during the following summer and not denied that Drexel was one of the original subscribers to the development. He bought the cottage on April 1, 1885, from one John D. Burke, who had bought it the same day from the Saratoga, Mt. McGregor and Lake George Railroad Company. Burke paid $500 for the cottage, and Drexel paid him the same amount. This double sale with no profit seems to have been a device to avoid any question that might come up over the sale of property by the corporation to one of its stockholders. Neither sale, oddly enough, was completed by the deed being "sealed and delivered" until after the death of General Grant. Technically, the cottage still belonged to the railroad company that summer. It seems fair to assume that Drexel bought the cottage to please Arkell and at the same time make a generous gesture to the general, and that he had little or no intention of using it himself.[3]

Arkell, rather than Drexel, made most of the arrangements. The New York Tribune reported on April 19 that "The Grant family decided yesterday to sell their cottage at Long Branch, and they will take the General to the Catskills this summer, if his health permits his removal from the city." Only a day or two later, Dr. Douglas denied this story. He said that "Gen. Grant would not go to the Catskills, even if he went out of the city." On April 26 the Tribune, telling of Grant's physical condition of the day before, said that "In the morning W. J. Arkell called and arranged definitely with the family for taking General Grant to Mount McGregor in the latter part of June or early

in July. . . . The cottage of Joseph W. Drexel, at Mount Mc-
Gregor, which has been tendered to General Grant, is large
enough to accommodate all the members of the family who
intend to accompany him." Mr. Drexel had given directions
that the cottage should be put in order at once for the Grant
family, and would "send a quantity of bric-a-brac and pictures
from his residence in this city to make it as pleasant as possible." [4]

When the move was made, a few weeks later, Dr. Douglas
gave the *Albany Evening Journal,* Arkell's newspaper, a statement of his reasons for accepting Drexel's offer. "I had intended," he said, "to have General Grant taken to a place where
the air was clear and pure and dry." The family had suggested
the cottage at Long Branch, which had been kept in Mrs.
Grant's name, but Douglas did not think the humid seacoast
atmosphere would be good for his patient. One day he made
the remark that, if he could find a place somewhere around
Saratoga, that above all would be his choice for a summer
home for the general. Shortly after, Colonel Grant told him
that he had an invitation to a place near Saratoga, on some
railroad. Douglas was a little puzzled, but that night the family
told him it was Mount McGregor. Douglas, who went to Saratoga every summer, knew the mountain and said at once, "That
is just the place I have been looking for. There is little heat
there, it is on the heights, it is free from vapors, and above all,
it is among the pines, and the pure air is especially grateful to
patients suffering as General Grant is suffering. So it happened
that just what we wanted we had." [5] Arkell's Hotel Balmoral,
readying for its second season as a Saratoga attraction, had been
paying good money to metropolitan journals for less effective
advertisements than this. The good doctor was unconsciously an
excellent promoter for the new resort.

When preparations were being made for Grant to leave the
city, the *Commercial Advertiser* described the place where he
planned to spend the summer. "The offer of Mr. Joseph W.
Drexel, a well-known gentleman of this city, and an old friend
of the General," had been accepted, it said:

Mr. Drexel has a Summer house at Saratoga, where he takes his family every year. Eleven miles north of Saratoga, on what is called Mount Mc-Gregor, Mr. Drexel has another cottage, which he is accustomed to use as it may suit his fancy. He was anxious that the General should come to his cottage at Saratoga, but it was decided that at Mount McGregor the retirement would be greater, and the keen, bracing mountain air would have a much better effect on his health. Consequently Mr. Drexel offered to the family the exclusive use of the McGregor cottage during the months of June and July. The offer was accepted, and the arrangements for conveying the sick man there are rapidly perfecting. . . .

The Drexel cottage is at a reasonable distance from other cottages and about a third of a mile from the hotel. It is of the Queen Anne style of architecture, two stories high, and contains about a dozen rooms. A wide piazza extends around three sides of the house. Mr. Drexel's idea was to have the cottage comfortable without making it luxurious. Gen. Grant's room will be in a corner of the house, on the first floor facing the piazza. There will be no steps to mount, and he can walk out on the verandas and enjoy the scenery. No food will be cooked in the house in order that the temperature may not be too high. The General and his family will receive their meals from the hotel.[6]

Dr. Douglas, according to the *Commercial Advertiser,* said that the tentative date of the move was June 24. The move would have been made sooner, but he thought the air on the mountain was still too cold. The actual move would depend on the general's condition, but would probably be between June 23 and July 1. Grant and his family were to stay at Mount McGregor through July, and perhaps longer. Dr. Douglas and his family were to accompany the party. Dr. Sands would be in readiness for a sudden call. Dr. Shrady and his family would go to their country place on the Hudson near Kingston, and he too would be within call in an emergency. A suite of rooms had been set aside for the Grant family at the Hotel Kaaterskill in the Catskills for the latter part of the summer.[7]

The growing heat in the city, and its effect on the general, hastened the move. Grant was depressed and feeble. Drs. Sands, Douglas, and Shrady had a consultation on June 14 and decided to have the patient taken away at once. The swelling in the neck had increased in size, they found, and infiltration had extended to the deep-seated tissues. The general's voice was much affected and he spoke with apparent effort. There was a difficulty in his breathing. Ulceration on the back of the throat and the side of the tongue was becoming active. From "the great and injurious effect the heat seemed to have upon the General," it appeared advisable to wait no longer. Grant seemed pleased at the decision.[8]

Meanwhile there had been much activity on Mount McGregor. "To fit the cottage for its expected guest it was necessary to repaint, paper, and furnish it throughout. . . . A fireplace in the reception room was also then constructed." All this was speedily accomplished, and the Grants found everything ready for them when they arrived ahead of schedule. A local correspondent of the New York *Evening Post,* visiting the place only a few days before the general's arrival, found the final touches being made: "To-day the agent of a firm of furnishers in New York is here putting things to rights. Full breakfast, dinner, and luncheon sets of Dresden, Minton, and glassware have arrived. . . ." The New York *World* had evidently sent a reporter to the mountain in advance, and described the cottage in considerable detail a day or two later. "The cottage," it said, "is a modest-looking two-story frame building, decked out in a new coat of old gold paint with neat brown trimmings." There was a wide veranda on three sides, and the cottage was surrounded by pines, maples, and oaks. The family or reception room had been artistically papered and veneered, and the ceiling paper was "radiant with gold stars." The doors and windows were painted light blue, and the brick fireplace was Tuscan red. The wrought-iron andirons bore griffin heads, "which glare savagely from behind a brass-trimmed firescreen."

This room was richly carpeted and held, in addition to the usual furniture, "a green cloth-covered mahogany writing-table." Folding doors separated it from the dining room, which had a heavy mahogany extension table, a dozen cane-bottomed chairs, and a mahogany sideboard. The general's sleeping room was furnished with a mahogany suite and wickerwork couch, rocker, and settee. An adjoining room would be occupied by Mrs. Grant. Another door led to Grant's servants' room. Two windows opened into the general's room from the west. They had "double shades, one cream colored the other black." The carpet was a delicate figured blue, and the paper was also of "a delicate mixed blue shade." There were six rooms on the second floor, reached by a staircase between the servants' and dining rooms. These were furnished with "ash, oak and mahogany suites." [9]

It was arranged for the general and his party to travel in a special train, made up of William H. Vanderbilt's private car, one other car, and a locomotive. "The car in which Gen. Grant will travel," the *World* said, "is fitted up most luxuriously and every detail which can add to his ease and comfort during the journey has been attended to." Mrs. Grant, her daughter Mrs. Nellie Sartoris, and Colonel and Mrs. Fred Grant were to go with the general. Dr. Douglas was to be at his side throughout the journey and during his stay on the mountain. Henry McQueeney, Grant's nurse, and Harrison Tyrrell, his valet, were to accompany him, and a maid would attend the ladies. [10]

The special train left Grand Central Station on the morning of June 16, and arrived in Saratoga Springs at 1:55 P.M. There had been a turnout of well-wishers at each station stop along the way, and at Saratoga the train was met by a line of applauding G.A.R. veterans in uniform. The Mount McGregor narrow-gage railroad tracks ran closely parallel to the main line for some distance, and the transfer from one train to the other was soon made. Before anyone could help him, the general stepped off his train, crossed to the Mount McGregor special car, and climbed up alone. This brought cheers from the crowd. Grant had been sleeping in an upholstered easy chair, since his choking attacks in the spring, with his feet on another chair. These bulky invalid chairs had been brought along, and now Colonel Fred and his helpers had hard work to get them through the door and into the little car. The general himself came out to supervise. On the car were J. W. Drexel, "General Grant's generous friend," and officials of the narrow-gage line— L. H. Fonda, the general manager, and John Kellogg, the director. "Mr. W. J. Arkell, one of the proprietors of the *Albany Evening Journal,* a projector of the General's trip to Mount McGregor," the *Commercial Advertiser* noted, "was thoughtfully attentive to all on the train over which he exercised supervision." He and Thomas Cable, the manager of the Hotel Balmoral, had accompanied the Grant family from New York.[11] There seem to have been reporters from almost all the metropolitan dailies as well.

It had been proposed to Grant to stop off at Mr. Drexel's house in Saratoga. "The heat there, however, was hardly less trying than at Albany, and the General wanted the trip over." The little engine started, and the climb up the mountain, "perhaps the most fatiguing part of Gen. Grant's journey," was finished at 2:40 P.M. In spite of the advertised solidity of the roadbed, reporters thought that it was a rough trip: "As the diminutive engine wheezed along the uneven rails up the steep grade she belched out clouds of stifling smoke which filled the car and gave the General much annoyance. Curve followed curve in quick succession and the car pitched from side to side like a boat in a stormy sea." [12]

When the train arrived at the "little platform which does duty as a station," there was a hospital cot waiting for the general. Grant ignored this and started walking up the hill toward the Drexel cottage. He tottered only a little way, however, passing under an arch which welcomed "Our Hero," and let himself be carried in a rattan chair. He walked up the steps of the cottage "with the sole assistance of his cane." After resting awhile on the porch, where Mrs. Drexel was present to receive him, he went inside and Harrison changed his clothes. He came out again in top hat and black coat and "sat for hours until the mosquitoes drove him in." Sam Willett, an Albany G.A.R. veteran, mounted guard before his door, telling reporters that he would stay on duty until the general left the mountains.[13] Arkell had presumably hired him, but this was never mentioned. When the general finally left the veranda, "he acknowledged the salute of a group of reporters with soldierly motion of his stick." Colonel Grant seemed elated with the results of the trip. His father had borne the fatigue much better than anyone had anticipated. He thought that the general would recover his speech fully and was hopeful of all-around improvement. Dr. Douglas, however, warned the newsmen that nothing more than a temporary improvement could be expected: "the decay of vitality is slowly but steadily progressing." [14]

Grant had a good rest that night, in spite of a thunderstorm. The next day was pleasantly cool and breezy, and he made "a supreme and memorable effort." He had been told of the fine view from a neighboring knoll, and walked there, leaning lightly on Harrison's arm and using his cane. He sat on a rustic bench admiring the view a short time, and then returned to the cottage. "The distance traversed was equal to about five city blocks," the *Herald*'s correspondent noted admiringly, "and is more continual walking than the General has done for several months past." He returned exhausted. After resting a while, he signaled for writing materials and wrote two notes, one for Dr. Douglas and the other labeled "Memoranda for my Family." Colonel Fred tore open the family letter at once, and found it rather alarming. "I feel that I am failing," it said, and went on to things that the general wanted taken care of. Douglas's note was equally depressing. In it Grant analyzed his symptoms carefully and said, "I can feel plainly that my system is preparing for dissolution." He made a rough calculation on when it might take place, and said that he did not want any more desperate efforts to save him. They only meant more suffering.[15] No one will ever know what dream of instant rejuvenation on the mountaintop may have evaporated from Grant's mind. The long walk had been a test, and his body had failed it.

The general probably did not realize just what the impact of these two matter-of-fact notes would be. The family were much excited, and "Mrs. Grant was almost prostrated." Dr. Douglas, admitting that he was worried by the general's expression of hopelessness, and fearing death by sudden exhaustion, telegraphed for Dr. Sands. Sands arrived on a special train the next morning only to find the patient sitting up and fully awake. He and Douglas examined Grant's throat and reported no immediate danger. Sands went back to New York the same afternoon and everyone relaxed. "It was like a calm after a storm." Meanwhile, Ulysses, Jr., and Jesse Grant, with Dr. Newman, had arrived. It was not the first time that the general had spoiled a death scene by refusing to lie down and play his part. He spent some time on the porch that afternoon, and stood to return the salutes of a group that marched past the cottage.[16]

Visitors soon began flocking to the mountain. As the biographer of Julia, Grant's devoted wife, has put it:

For the time being Mount McGregor was the most conspicuous spot in the world, for the General had traveled in every country and his story was assuming the proportions of a classical tragedy. Here was a great public figure watching himself die. He knew what he had. He knew what the papers were saying. He was a witness to his own agony as well as being its subject. Enemy voices were stilled at last. The peaks and abysses of his career were all in view, but catalyzed in his final show of courage.[17]

For the most part the visitors who came up the mountain on the busy little train, by carriage, or on foot, were respectful as well as sympathetic. Every afternoon long lines of them would walk past the cottage. Now and then Grant, sitting on the porch on sunny afternoons, writing or reading the newspapers, would look up and nod or wave his hand. Sam Willett, the G.A.R. veteran who had constituted himself Grant's guard and had pitched a tent behind the cottage, spent part of his time playing with the Grant grandchildren and Dr. Douglas's two little girls, and the rest keeping unwanted visitors away. Usually no one attempted to reach the porch, but he posted himself at the foot of the steps to prevent it.[18]

Sometimes Willett was not there when the train came in, and sometimes callers were expected. Quite likely he was occasionally overawed by an imposing front. One afternoon, shortly after Grant's arrival, a couple of prominent local citizens came up on the porch and insisted on talking affably to him at great length. Finally the general went in. Colonel Grant followed at once, to see if he was wanted, and his father wrote on a tablet, "They will talk me to death if I stay out here." He stayed inside until the visitors took the train and went back to Saratoga. Colonel Fred, whose public relations sense was usually on the alert, incautiously showed the slip of paper to a reporter and the story was out. The colonel, embarrassed, took the first opportunity to tell the press that "it was the desire of the family to save the General from the common run of visitors, but that he was pleased to see Judge Hilton and Dr. Gray, neither of whom annoyed him." The story, nevertheless, served a good purpose; there were fewer social inflictions.[19]

It was soon known that Grant was still working on his book. N. E. Dawson, the stenographer supplied by Charles L. Webster & Co., had accompanied him to the mountain, "to assist him in revising the last proofs of his book." It became apparent that this revision would be extensive. Within three days of his arrival, the general indicated that he wanted Fred to attend to some details on the publication, and the next day he wrote a paragraph for insertion in the book. The next day he wrote more. The family took this as an encouraging sign. He began sitting out on the porch, well wrapped up, and writing with pad and pencil almost every day for considerable periods. "It was interesting to watch this literary labor on the part of the great captain from the piazza of the hotel that looked down into the cottage," the *Herald*'s reporter said, "and see how good an example in earnestness of purpose and concentration of thought this very sick man was setting to his able-bodied literary brethren." "The common feeling often expressed," said the *Tribune,* "is that General Grant never fought as well as he fights now. A clerical-looking man, who looked at him from a respectable distance, said that it was the most eloquent and suggestive sermon that he had ever met with." [20]

As proofs came up from New York, Colonel Fred, one of his brothers, or stenographer Dawson read them to the general and collected the revision slips that he wrote. The room next to

Grant's at the corner of the cottage, first intended for Mrs. Grant's use, was almost at once made into an office, while Julia moved upstairs. At night Fred and Dawson wrote the revisions into the proofs. Lights sometimes burned in the office for hours after the general had gone to bed, reporters noticed. Sometimes "Col. Fred and Stenographer Dawson could be seen through the windows busy with charts and war records, from which they were carefully verifying the manuscript for the General's book." It was speculated whether their low conversation did not occasionally keep him awake.[21]

Grant's voice had almost completely failed, and his writing, even his side of a conversation, was normally in the form of notes written on a pad. The process had become tedious to him, and the mere effort of writing a tax on his strength. Then on a cool day when he was sitting by the fire in the living room, the general astonished everyone. He had Dawson collect all the slips he had written in the last day or two, studied them for a time, and summoned the stenographer to him. "Then, as the proof sheets were slowly read over, he stopped the reading at different points and dictated short insertions." It was estimated that he dictated, in a whisper, enough material to add nearly ten printed pages to his book. He had not done so much work for weeks before leaving New York. That night the general wrote a whimsical little note to Dr. Douglas, apparently after he had tried to speak and not been understood: "I said that I had been adding to my book and to my coffin. I presume every strain of the mind or body is one more nail in the coffin." The little joke was wasted on Douglas, who took it sadly. A little later he wrote again, "I have worked off all that I had notes of, and which often kept me thinking at night. I will not push to make more notes for the present." Nevertheless, the next morning Grant sat in the parlor and wrote for nearly an hour "and revised some proof sheets of his book." [22]

Douglas became uneasy after the dictation episode. All of the general's relapses, he told the press, had followed such unusual efforts. He had already written Dr. Shrady, asking him to come up to the mountain for consultation, and Shrady arrived the following day. The medical men gave out that the general's condition was better than it would have been if he had stayed in New York, but they did not want to be understood as saying that the disease had been checked. Dr. Shrady stayed at the house, relieving Douglas for the night, and he and the general had a long talk, the general writing his part of the conversation.[23]

Shrady asked Grant how he had been progressing with his book. "I have dictated only twenty pages since I have been here," the general wrote, "and written out with my own hand about as much more. I have no connected account now to write. Occasionally I see something that suggests a few remarks." Shrady made a protest over his using his voice too much, and said that absolute rest gave him a chance in the future. Grant wrote in reply, a little pathetically, "I do not suppose I will ever have my voice back again at all strong." [24]

Shrady the next day sent a long report by telegraph to the *Medical Record* on Grant's condition, for use in its next issue. He noted the gradual progress of the disease, but also that "The removal to Mt. McGregor has so far proved beneficial." That same day was made the photograph of Grant completing the *Personal Memoirs* that has become famous and been many times reproduced:

> Mount McGregor, June 25.—Visitors here to-day saw how Gen. Grant looks in the sick room. He came out on the porch about noon in his gown and blue skull cap. A pillow at the back of his chair reached far above his head. A shawl, fastened to the pillow, covered the right side of his face and neck where the glandular swelling is. The swelling was further protected by a scarf which muffled him closely. The thermometer marked 80°, but he was wrapped from waist to feet in a thick robe. While he was thus enjoying the air and sunshine a photographer got permission to go on the porch and level a camera on him. He sat outdoors for nearly four hours altogether. Dr. Shrady, who stops at the cottage, was with him part of the time.
>
> The general was quite active with his pencil and seemed in good spirits.[25]

That evening a Bath chair, the gift of an admirer, arrived at the cottage. The next day Shrady and the family prepared a surprise for the general, promising him a ride. When he came out at eleven o'clock he found not a horse and carriage but, to his astonishment, "a little black buggy top on wheels at the foot of the porch steps." There was a single tongue with a crosspiece near the end, like the handle of a child's cart, and a rod along the rear by which the thing might be pushed. The ladies laughed while the general took in the contraption. He got into it and Harrison, taking the handle, started up the steep path toward the hotel. Douglas went along, and commandeered a small boy to push. At the hotel Grant climbed the steps unaided and sat in a chair. Someone asked him if he wanted the Bath chair brought up on the porch. "He said he guessed his horse wouldn't run away." Later the chair was brought up, and he made a tour of the long hotel porch in it. That afternoon Shrady started home. In the evening Douglas said that this had been Grant's best day yet.[26]

The general had to pay for his fun. That night he slept badly. Mucous accumulations brought on coughing and expectorating, weakening him. Douglas, who had gone to the hotel, was summoned. The recent improvement had been arrested. The next day, which was hot and close, added to Grant's discomfort, and he did not leave his room until afternoon. He wrote a note to Douglas saying that he felt worse than he had for some time. "My mouth hurts and cocaine ceases to give the relief it did." The Bath chair was not even mentioned. He sat in his usual place at the corner of the porch, "reading for the most part and indulging in pencil talk with his friends and family." Dr. Newman, a great believer in the power of prayer, who had been away and come back the day before, said he was "at last forced to the conclusion that nothing short of a miracle could now help the General." [27]

The Grant family had always been very close. The relation between the general and Julia was one of complete devotion on both sides. "The days went by for Julia in muted sorrow," says her biographer. "She dared not show him how she felt and add

to his discomfort." He would not let her take part in the nurs-
ing. Harrison cared for him during the day and Henry at night,
but Julia was at his side as soon as he wakened in the morning.
She "talked to him in her old gay way and told him stories, then
moved into another room to hide her tears." She was alert to
every variation in his condition. Reporters noticed that when
he was on the porch her chair was usually close to his. She was
somewhere in view whenever he appeared.[28]

Fred Grant's two children, Julia and Ulysses 3rd, were looked
after by Louise, their French nurse. They were whisked over to
the hotel in times of crisis, but on good days they were always
welcomed beside the general's chair. "Almost up to the end it
made him happy to have his family gather around him on the
porch." More than once, on good days, he put on his silk hat
and the family posed around him for group photographs. "He
was proud of the solid clan that he and Julia had founded, and
at the devotion his children gave him. They all played their part
to the finish." [29] The entire household at first took their meals
at the cottage, the hotel sending over the food. The disadvan-
tages and inconveniencies of this plan brought a change toward
the end of June. A large parlor was set aside for the private
use of the Grant family at the hotel. The general, of course,
continued to sip "his milk and egg and beef tea" in his room.[30]

The Clemens (Mark Twain) family usually went to Elmira
for the summer. This year they did not go until June 27. The
next day Twain had a summons saying that the general had
asked to see him. He went to Mount McGregor at once and
spent several days there. He found Grant still working on the
book, though very feeble. Grant wanted to talk about it, and
Mark carried away with him a package of slips of paper from
the general's side of the conversation. One read: "There is much
more that I could do if I was a well man. I do not write quite as
clearly as I could if well. If I could read it over myself many
little matters of anecdote and incident would suggest themselves
to me." Another: "Have you seen any portion of the second
volume? It is up to the end, or nearly so. As much more work
as I have done to-day will finish it. I have worked faster than if

I had been well. I have used my three boys and a stenographer."
Still another: "If I could have two weeks of strength I could
improve it very much. As I am, however, it will have to go
about as it is, with verifications by the boys and by suggestions
which will enable me to make a point clear here and there." [31]

Once he asked if an estimate could now be made of what his
family would get from the publication. Twain told him promptly
that more than 100,000 sets had been sold; Grant's share, secured by safe bonds, was more than $150,000. This gave the
general deep comfort, but Mark said that the country was not
yet more than one-third canvassed. The returns should be twice
as much more by the end of the year. Grant made no further
inquiry, and probably never mentioned the subject again to anyone.[32] Mark Twain's presence on the mountain did not escape
notice. The *Sun*'s reporter, describing Grant's day on July 1,
said that "Mark Twain came here yesterday, and is still here.
He spends most of the time at the cottage." The next day the
Evening Post's reporter described the office, which was "occupied by Colonel Grant, a stenographer, and others who have
charged themselves with responsibility for the literary correct-
ness of the General's recollections of the war." He added the
surprising fact that "Samuel L. Clemens and Colonel Grant
worked together nearly all night on the proofs of the second
volume. Colonel Grant said to the writer that he did not go to
bed till after daylight this morning." That afternoon Colonel
Fred was busy packing up proofs and maps of battles to send
to the publishers. "The work," he said, "is finished so far as
we have to do with it." "Mr. Clemens," the reporter concluded, "left the mountain this morning satisfied that the second
volume was ready for the press. He is understood to be the
responsible publisher of the work." [33]

How much of the material that Mark Twain and Colonel
Fred checked over in their night's work was actually proof, and
how much was new manuscript, it would be hard to say. Much
of the second volume had just been rewritten. They were both
unquestionably eager to get the book put to bed, but neither
could really have believed when Mark left the mountain that

this had been done. They knew that the general was still writing, and would have more to say if he was able to say it. The *Commercial Advertiser* got the impression that such work would be minimal. "Col. Fred. Grant tells me," its correspondent recorded on the day that Mark Twain left, "that the first volume of his father's work is already in press, and that the second volume is now in the same condition that the first was two months ago. Gen. Grant's part of the work is really over except an occasional correction." [34]

There was no love lost between Dr. Newman and the skeptical Mark Twain. Shortly after he left Mount McGregor, Twain dictated some observations on the minister. Mrs. Grant had summoned Newman, he said, from California, where he had got $10,000 for a funeral sermon, "no doubt worth the money." Newman came and began his ministrations at the general's bedside, and, if one could believe his daily reports, Grant "had conceived a new and perfect interest in things spiritual." Twain said it was fair to presume that most of these reports originated in Newman's own imagination. "Col. Fred told me that his father was, in this matter, what he was in all matters and at all times—that is to say perfectly willing to have family prayers going on, or anything else that would be satisfactory to anybody, or increase anybody's comfort in any way." But while his father was a good man, the colonel added, "and indeed as good as any man, Christian or otherwise, he was *not* a praying man." Some incredible speeches had been put in Grant's mouth by Dr. Newman, Twain observed. There are notes written by the general in his last days that seem to show Newman's efforts as not entirely wasted—a pious phrase here and there—but he admitted in his diary that he could never persuade Grant to take communion or to leave behind him "some immortal saying of his relations to Christ." [35]

While Twain was still at Mount McGregor, the general wrote what amounted to a whole new chapter, to be added to the one on Appomattox. Newman had gone to the cottage on the afternoon of July 1, expecting to find him weak, but Grant was a man of surprises. "I asked him about it," Newman told a reporter. Evidently the general was nettled by this tactless inquiry. "He wrote that he didn't know he was weak, and that during the day, without a rest for his arm, he had worked for four hours, writing enough to make a new chapter for his book. He had remembered omitting to say anything about several generals, and had put down his estimate of them." The next day he wrote again, doing nearly as much work, giving his estimate of a number of persons in civil life. "It is intended to make a new chapter of military men and civilians with whom he was brought in contact during the war," the *New York Times* said.[36]

It was also during this burst of activity that Grant wrote the preface to his book, beginning, " 'Man proposes and God disposes.' There are but few important events in the affairs of men brought about by their own choice." It reviewed the history of the book project briefly, and apologized for the work not being done better. "I have used my best efforts, with the aid of my eldest son, F. D. Grant, assisted by his brothers, to verify from the records every statement of fact given. The comments are my own, and show how I saw the matters treated of whether others saw them in the same light or not." He asked no favor in presenting the volumes to the public, but hoped they would meet the approval of the reader. The preface was signed, "U. S. Grant, Mount McGregor, New-York, July 1, 1885." The publishers gave it to the press a few days later. In editorial comment the *New York Tribune* praised the frankness and simplicity of the preface. "In his modesty and candor," said the *Tribune,* "the General feels compelled to apologize to his readers for what he considers serious defects in his work," and that he might have done better if he had had more time. "The patient sufferer at Mount McGregor needs to feel no uneasiness on that score. Never did an author submit his work to a more sympathetic and indulgent circle of readers." [37]

Notes written by the general to Colonel Fred at this time, and carefully saved by the Grant family, illustrate both the method of work and the hope that the general had of helping to heal the wounds of sectionalism with his book. They show, too, that Badeau's place had not been fully supplied. In one he said:

This illustration of the Grant family at Mount McGregor is from the front page of Frank Leslie's Illustrated Newspaper, *July 25, 1885. In the picture (left to right) are U. S. Grant, Jr., Mrs. U. S. Grant, Mrs. Sartoris (Grant's daughter Nellie), General Grant (seated center), Mrs. Fred Grant and two children, Colonel Fred Grant, Mrs. Jesse Grant and child, and Jesse Grant. The children are, from left to right, Julia, Ulysses 3rd, and Nellie. In the lower left is a small drawing of the exterior of the Drexel cottage where Grant stayed during June and July until his death on the 23rd. In the lower right is a facsimile of one of the many notes the general wrote after it became increasingly difficult and ultimately impossible for him to talk.—Courtesy of General Research and Humanities Division; The New York Public Library; Astor, Lenox and Tilden Foundations*

"I want what I wrote yesterday for chapter 'In Conclusion' about 'change of feeling between north and south having started in the expression of sympathy by all classes and sections of people for me.' Someone who has not the partiality of the family should be consulted." In another: "Where are you in the review now? When is Buck [Ulysses, Jr.] coming up again? I begin to feel anxious about the review of the second volume. There may be more difficulty in placing all the parts than we think." Again: "What part are you reading up and verifying? Will you be sending anything to the printer this week?—final vol. of course. When Buck comes I think he will stay until you are through. It will be a good thing to get the second vol. finished as soon as possible. The edition is so large that it will be impossible to get the book out at the time expected. If the plates were ready now it would be a difficult job." Still another: "It seems to me that I got the campaign about Petersburg and the move to Appomattox pretty good on the last attempt. How many pages will there be besides appendix? What in 2 vol. Have you compared much of the 2nd vol. with other writers. Leave out the incident of Mrs. Tyler after Spottsylvania. I should change Spotts. if I was able and could improve N. Ana and Cold Harbor." Considerately in another: "Fred, if you feel the least unwell do not work until you feel like it. Your services are too important now to have you break down." [38]

Badeau, who had not believed in the spring that Grant could finish the book without his help, later admitted that the general had showed a remarkable burst of activity in "the fresh and reviving air of his new situation," and had "resumed his literary labor with extraordinary energy for a man in his condition." While Badeau was not with Grant at Mount McGregor, he said, "I know that his effort there must have been prodigious. He dictated or composed more matter in the eight weeks after the 1st of May than in any other eight weeks of his life; while in the eight weeks immediately preceding that date he did not compose as many pages." [39]

Badeau was not at Mount McGregor, but his shadow was. Mark Twain had a phobia on the subject of literary piracy.

There was no international copyright agreement, and as early as April he had warned Webster to keep all proof sheets of the Grant book in his safe at night. Until the day of issue, he said, a Canadian emissary would be snooping around seeking to buy or steal proof sheets. "No book ever stood in such peril as this one," he declared. "Long before it is out thieves & bribers will be thick around the printing houses & binderies, ready to buy or steal even a couple of pages & sell to somebody." He was going to have to borrow $200,000 before issue; "then if a Canadian edition comes over the border ahead of us, it is lost." He seems to have infected Fred Grant, and finally the general himself, with the same fear. Rumors reached them early in June that Badeau had had offers to get out a pirated edition of the *Personal Memoirs*. "At first he was so incredulous of that report that he would not address Gen. Badeau about it," Colonel Grant told a *Times* reporter later, "thinking that it would be an insult to him." But at Mount McGregor he did remodel the first volume of the book to defeat any possible piracy or perversion. "Essential changes were made pursuant to this new plan." As far as Badeau was concerned, they need have had no fears. He was preparing another book about Grant, but it was his own and it was an honest and admiring book. But Mark Twain's fear was not without substance; a little later Charles L. Webster & Co. warned the public that "Numerous cheap imitations of the book are now hawked about the country." [40]

The work of the last few days had taken its toll, and Grant was weary. He tried to take a nap on his cot, but the prone position brought on a violent coughing fit and alarmed the family. Noticing their anxiety, he put on a good front and had Harrison take him up to the hotel and back in the Bath chair. Afterward he had another coughing spell, and Douglas sent for Dr. Sands. Plans for a Fourth of July celebration were canceled. Sands came up on the fourth and, after consultation with Douglas, returned to New York. The doctors found no material change since Shrady had left, but Grant was growing noticeably weaker. They told him frankly that exhaustion would doubtless be the final result. There were a number of visitors at the cottage on the holiday. Ex-Senator Chaffee arrived that day. He had not seen Grant for many weeks, and found him much weaker. He was reminded that he had once thought the disease was not cancer. He admitted that there was no doubt about it now in his mind; that "the diagnosis of the doctors was right." [41]

The next day Grant was reported as cheerful and better after a good night. Dr. Douglas said at breakfast that he, too, had enjoyed a night of better rest than he had taken in a long time. It was a "perfect Sabbath day," and many visitors came to the mountain to watch the general sitting on the porch reading the New York Sunday papers. "The last week's work on the book

With General Grant (who is seated, center) in this group at Mount McGregor are Mrs. Grant (far left), their daughter Nellie Sartoris (between Mrs. Grant and the general), Colonel Fred Grant and his wife Ida (both standing). Seated on the steps from left to right are Mrs. Jesse Grant and the three Grant grandchildren, U. S. Grant 3rd, his sister Julia (later Princess Cantacuzene), and their cousin Nellie.—Courtesy of The Rutherford B. Hayes Library, Fremont, Ohio

had so ended," the *Tribune* said, "that the General to-day felt much relieved as to its progress." "To-day he learned that he had written about two hundred more pages for his book than were absolutely necessary for its completion," according to the *Herald*, "and that all that was to be done to make this a finished work was the reading of the galley proofs." Evidently Webster or Twain had sent up the word, in an effort to shut off the flow and get the second volume into the presses.[42]

Several days passed quietly, Grant spending most of the time in his room and making only occasional inquiries about the progress on the proofs. On the late afternoon of July 6 he wrote a note to Dr. Douglas, who had just returned from an errand to Saratoga, having previously given his patient an injection of

The Grant and Douglas children. Dr. Douglas's two daughters and General Grant's grandchildren played together at Mount McGregor during the summer of 1885. The children from left to right are Harriet Sheldon Douglas; U. S. Grant 3rd, who died a retired major general in 1968; Julia Grant, later Princess Cantacuzene; Josephine Douglas; and Nellie Grant.—Courtesy of Mrs. Lee Gwynne Martin

morphine: "The injection worked very well, and I hope at not too great a cost. The pain left me entirely so that it was an enjoyment to lay awake. I did get asleep, however, from the mere absence of pain, and woke up a short time before four." Pain was his close comrade. He sometimes refused cocaine, however, telling Douglas that the relief it gave was only temporary but the "injury done" was fed and kept up by it. By this, Douglas said, "he meant to indicate the tendency of this drug to impair the vocal powers and destroy the voice." Douglas did not dismiss this as a mere sick fancy. The use of cocaine as a painkiller was relatively new, and Grant probably knew as much about its effects as anybody. The disease was following its natural course, the doctor told reporters. The end would probably be by simple exhaustion; "all probabilities of a death by choking, so much feared by the General, have now passed away." [43]

Visitors had been kept away for a time, but July 8 was a day of social activity. The day was warm and fresh, and Grant was up and sitting on the porch by eleven o'clock. A group of ladies came on the afternoon train to call on the family, and the general seemed pleased to have them there. Following them a Catholic priest from Baltimore came up on the porch and introduced himself, saying, "We are all praying for you, Gen. Grant." The general motioned him to be seated, and wrote a graceful note of acknowledgment, signing and dating it. Later a large group of editors from the Mexican Associated Press, who were touring the country, came in a body. They went to the hotel first and conferred with Colonel Fred, but the general sent word that he would be greatly pleased to see them. They were all formally presented and shook his hand. Grant seemed highly gratified at their visit and wrote them a note referring to the expulsion of the French from Mexico. He predicted that Mexico, with its splendid resources, would soon develop greatly. [44]

The book was still uppermost in his mind, however. That same day he wrote a letter to Julia, which was found in his pocket after his death. In it he made some recommendations for her action following that event, and specified a number of bequests as soon as receipts justified them. "For the last few days,"

General Grant shown working on his memoirs on the porch of the Drexel cottage at Mount McGregor. This illustration appeared in Century Magazine, *July 1908.—Courtesy of General Research and Humanities Division; The New York Public Library; Astor, Lenox and Tilden Foundations*

he added, "although my suffering has not been as intense as heretofore, that my end is approaching rapidly *I earnestly pray and desire*. I am sure I never will leave Mt. McGregor alive. I pray God however that it may be spared to complete the necessary work upon my book. Should I dye there will be a funeral and a breakup here. The review of the book for the printer will be suspended until fall. The subscriptions are so large that it can not be got out at the stipulated time even if there is no detention. But for these considerations I would welcome the arrival of the 'Messenger of Peace', the earlier the better." [45]

Douglas was distressed at the social strain to which his patient had submitted that day, and said that "the little strength that he had gained during the previous forty-eight hours he had lost." Telegrams were sent out to a number of prominent people that he was too weak to receive them. The next day, however, Grant did receive two callers. One of them was Charles Wood, of Lansingburg, who had sent the general a check for $1,000 when he learned of the failure of Grant & Ward. The check was "for services rendered to the nation up to April 9, 1865." The other visitor was Robert U. Johnson of the *Century*. Johnson had come to confer with Colonel Grant about the remaining articles for the magazine, and had not expected to see the general, but the colonel voluntarily arranged for Johnson to see him.[46]

While Johnson himself had given out early in March, when Grant was presumably dying, that the articles were finished and revised, there were important points to settle about their use. The Century Company intended to use them in their later war book, as well as in the magazine, and Mark Twain relied on them as a basic part of the *Personal Memoirs*. He found that there was only a verbal understanding between Grant and the Century Company permitting him to use the articles in his book, and was disturbed. Grant was too sick to write them over again. Twain had Colonel Grant write down what he understood the agreement to be, the general signed it, and Mark took it to the Century office. He found Roswell Smith and the editors in agreement, and this difficulty was settled. The Wilderness article, however, proved to be in rough draft only, and unfinished. The Century Company "called several times to get the fourth article, offending Col. Fred Grant," Mark Twain said, "as they knew his father was considered to be dying." One day while Badeau was still at the house, Mark saw a pile of typed manuscript on the siege of Vicksburg that ran to nearly 20,000 words. Badeau said that it was the Vicksburg article for the *Century*. Twain argued that it made two ordinary articles, and that Grant had fulfilled his agreement. The *Century* had no right to insist on another article. This argument made no impression on the Century people at first. Later an agreement was reached, by which the Vicksburg article was to be cut sharply, most of the detail on the campaign being given up for exclusive use in the *Personal Memoirs*. Johnson, who had to do the cutting, was bitterly resentful, especially as *Century*'s readers had been promised the material from Grant's hand. Webster had got the general to ask the favor, after some miscalculation on the makeup of the first volume. "It is a preposterous request," Johnson told Buel, but he went ahead with what he regarded as a brutal multilation.[47]

In the interview with the general, Johnson, who had only recently completed this disagreeable task, was all politeness. "As he could communicate only in writing," he remembered later, "I did the talking, merely conveying the sympathy of my associates and the assurance that we should gladly do anything we could for the success of the book in Mr. Clemens's hands, adjusting our plans to his. I told the General that we had willingly acceded to his son's wish that we should relinquish that part of the long Vicksburg narrative that preceded the siege—an article in itself." Grant smiled faintly and bowed his acknowledgment. "I could hardly keep back the tears as I made my farewell to the great soldier who had saved the Union for all its people," Johnson recalled, "and to the man of warm and courageous heart who had fought his last long battle for those he so tenderly loved." At about the same time, the Century Company voluntarily sent Grant a check for $1,500, as additional payment for the articles. Grant was pleased, and had Colonel Fred write that "he feels gratified in having done business with men who have always acted the part of gentlemen." [48]

Another caller, whose visit the next day gave Grant particular pleasure, was ex-Confederate General Simon B. Buckner, his one-time West Point classmate and later opponent at Fort Donelson. Reporters buzzed about Buckner as he left, but he said that he couldn't tell them what was said without Grant's permission: "The visit was purely personal." After he got back to New York, Buckner learned that the general was eager to have the interview given to the public, as it might add to good

General Grant and some of his family at Mount McGregor. Adults, left to right, are Mrs. Jesse Grant, Mrs. Nellie Sartoris, General Grant, Dr. Douglas, Fred Grant and wife Ida. The grandchildren are, left to right, Nellie, Julia, and Ulysses 3rd. This illustration appeared in Harper's Weekly, *June 27, 1885.—Courtesy of The New-York Historical Society, New York City*

will between the sections. Buckner pulled out and read to reporters the slips of paper on which Grant had written his part
of the conversation, beginning, "I have witnessed since my sickness just what I have wished to see ever since the war—harmony
and good feeling between the sections." Grant had told Douglas
that he was willing to pay the price for this gratifying interview,
but Dr. Newman, who could never confine himself to his own
professional field, now gave it as his opinion that it was time
to issue "an imperative edict" against such strains on the general's strength. "The difficulty with this suggestion," the *Herald*
reporter noted, "is that the General's anxiety to see his friends
gets the better of his judgment sometimes." [49] Mark Twain paid
his last visit, evidently a brief one, arriving as Buckner left. No
record has been found of his conversation with Grant at this
time, but they undoubtedly talked about the book. The general
probably told him substantially what he wrote to Douglas on
the same day, a note that Douglas dated July 10, 11:30 A.M.:
"Buck has brought up the last of first vol. in print. In two weeks
if they work hard they can have the second vol. copied ready to
go to the printer. *I will then feel that my work is done.*" [50]

The printed sheets, or page proofs, were sent back to the publisher the very next day, while Colonel Grant and Dawson went
on making a finished longhand copy of the revised manuscript
for the second volume. Colonel Grant told a reporter that day
that there had been much progress in the work in the last week,
and the book itself would not be long in making its appearance.
"The delay," he was quoted as saying, "has arisen principally
because of his father's inability to read the proof as fast as it
was offered to him." Grant had been given little if any opportunity to read this last batch, and the colonel's remark has a
hollow ring to it. What was delaying the book was not the general's slowness in reading the proof, but what he did after he
had had it read to him. Like Winston Churchill many years
later, he simply could not leave it alone. Extensive revision in
page proofs is calculated to drive any publisher mad, and there
is plenty of evidence that Charles L. Webster & Co. was in a
hurry for finished copy. [51]

Just after the general's death the *New York Times* reviewed the writing of the *Personal Memoirs,* evidently getting its information from Colonel Grant. It noted that it might puzzle those who recalled the announcement of the completion of Grant's book early in June, that there were frequent references from Mount McGregor later of continued work on the book. It might have been considered completed if the general had died then, the *Times* said, but he wanted to revise the organization and "he felt and often said that he could work profitably on it every day up to the time of its publication, if he had strength enough." When he had exhausted his notes, he went on writing as suggestions occurred to him, "but the main work was cutting out anecdotes that might hurt individuals." The manuscript was 200 pages over the contract, and some cutting could well be done, but good things were being destroyed in this way. "To such corrections and to other alterations in the proofs the Colonel and Mr. Dawson attended. By their diligence all the revised proofs for the first volume of the work were mailed to the publishers on July 11. That was a great relief to all, for the General's mind could not be quieted on that part of the book until it was beyond his reach." [52]

In effect, Colonel Grant, trying desperately to meet the publisher's demands for finished copy, and to persuade his father to relax, took his book away from him. With the first volume in New York, and with the revised second volume being pieced together and put in fair longhand copy for the printer, there was nothing much for the general to do. Dawson said later that on this date, "at last he had reached the end of all he could do," although "He had intended to have the whole read over to him and to have revised it all." The evidence is that he had reached the end of all that his son and the doctors, no doubt in close collusion, would let him do. Grant seems to have accepted the decision without argument. He did nothing that day requiring physical or mental exertion. He admitted to Dr. Newman that he had overdone it in receiving his Mexican visitors, and had not got his strength back. Douglas said that the general's determination to be quiet had brought a decided improvement in his condition. An undated note from the general to Colonel Fred was quite likely written at this time. It indicates that Grant had given up his own work, that there was still much to be done on the book, and that he wanted nothing to interfere with its completion:

If I should die here make arrangements for embalming my body and retaining it for buryal until pleasant weather in the fall. In that case you can continue your work and insure its being ready as fast as the printers can take it. This is my great interest in life, to see my work done. There is nothing in my condition that I know of except presentiment, on account of weakness to indicate that I may not as well live for the next three months as for the last five. Do *not* let the memory of me interfere with the progress of the book.[53]

Grant had no doubt exhausted himself by his heavy social schedule of recent days, and Douglas was overtaxed in caring for him. Shrady was asked to come to his relief for a few days. Shrady came on July 13, just after the general began to rally, briefly but amazingly. He began to use his voice again, quite distinctly, his pulse was strong and regular, and he swallowed his liquid food without apparent pain. Dr. Newman had preached a Sunday sermon on the piazza of the Hotel Balmoral the day before, and the general had come out on the cottage porch where he could listen to the singing of familiar hymns. Governor David Hill, with Mr. Drexel and Mr. Arkell, walked down to the cottage after the service and spent a few minutes with him. "He wrote that he did not feel as much of an invalid as he looked." When Mrs. Sartoris came back from the hotel he asked her, in an almost clear voice, "Well, Nellie, did you have a good sermon to-day?" The next morning he carried on all his conversation with Dr. Douglas orally, and told him he felt like going to work. Douglas dissented, but the general did write for nearly an hour in the forenoon. "The present remarkable change in Gen. Grant's condition," Douglas told reporters, "is one of those strange phases of temporary improvement that is characteristic of cancerous disease"; how long it might continue neither he nor anyone could tell. That afternoon he turned his patient over to Shrady and went to take a well-earned rest.[54]

Before Douglas relinquished his authority, evidently upset by the general's rebelliousness, he announced a policy of absolute quiet. Shrady immediately confirmed the policy. "During this week special efforts will be made to secure perfect quiet for the General, in order to continue if possible the present favorable conditions." The general, it was given out, was "disposed to aid this experiment in every way, and, though it will be a severe trial to him to abstain from that which, in his lonely life, has been a source of great pleasure, he will not frustrate the purpose of his physicians by any transgression of their orders." Thus, rather pompously, General Grant's final surrender was announced. This time he really had given up. That night Dr. Douglas, theoretically on vacation, helped to dress the general's throat and prepare him for bed. He asked the general what kind of day he had had, and Grant answered, "Quiet, almost too quiet." [55]

The next day was quiet, though the general spent about two hours on the porch in the afternoon. He had complained a little of muscular weakness in the morning, but Shrady thought this was only subjective, as weakness did not appear either in his pulse or his appearance. The doctor noticed, however, that "The General misses the opportunity which his book gave him of occupying his mind." He was getting a little restive under "this enforced quietude and entire freedom from all occupation." On that day Grant gave Douglas a long note that made this clear. He said that he had been given the time that he wanted to work on his book "so that the authorship would be clearly mine." His work had been done hastily the first time, and much had been left out. He "did all of it over again from the crossing of the Rapidan River in June/64 [*sic*] to Appomattox," and since then had added as much as 50 pages to the book. "There is nothing more I should do to it now, and therefore I am not likely to be more ready to go than at this moment." [56]

Douglas doubtless showed the note to Shrady. Grant had benefited from the enforced rest of the last few days, but "he had rested out and become tired of doing nothing." Mental activity had become habitual with him. "The prospect of doing something on his book, so long as that remained, fed his mind and kept alive his desire to rouse himself for a definite object," the doctors told the press. Now he felt the want of occupation. "He retired for the night disquieted, because he thought the day had gone for nothing, although he considered himself well able to have worked." "There is reason to believe," said the *Herald,* "that yesterday he expressed himself very strongly to one of his physicians in reference to this enforced quietude and intimated that he would prefer an immortal quietude to a lengthened continuance of it." Enforced idleness was obviously growing irksome to him, and the physicians "thought some means of interesting his thoughts may prove advisable." They relaxed their regulations against mental activity, and suggested reading to him. Colonel Grant told him that the *Century* wanted him to do an article on a civil subject. Shrady advised him to read *The Autocrat of the Breakfast Table,* and Mrs. Grant promptly ordered the book. "There is a brilliant mental occupation for him," Douglas told reporters; "the *Century* magazine has invited his opinion in a short article on the limit of the Presidential term." This and other tasks, of course, depended on the general's humor, but they offered a "means of relieving him of the dispiriting impression that nothing more is left for him to do." The fact was, the *Herald* commented, that since the general had completed the writing of his book, "life has become, despite his very pleasant surroundings, somewhat of a burden to him." [57]

Shrady's visits for consultation with Douglas, and to relieve him briefly, evidently gave the general pleasure. Shrady enjoyed a joke and, for all his professional skill and tireless devotion, the solemn presence of Douglas must sometimes have been a bore. This time Shrady left Mount McGregor on July 18. Grant seemed anxious to know when he would come again, and said he would like to have the doctor with him "at the last." Shrady told him that he would surely be within call, but did not think at the time that the final summons would come as soon as it did. [58]

Grant did not appear to take much interest in the *Century* proposal, but seemed inclined to perfect quiet. He spent most of July 19 on the porch of the cottage, "sitting well bundled up in his willow chair." "He read the newspapers and altogether passed a restful and uneventful day." The last known photograph of the general was taken on this day, with the general scanning a newspaper, his cane on an adjacent chair, and the faithful Harrison on the alert just inside the door. Douglas told reporters that night that the disease was not at the moment spreading, and weakness seemed to be the factor most to be considered. "Growing weaker day by day, as the General has been doing now for some days past, will inevitably lead to the end," he said, "and that is not very far off." [59]

The next day was much the same until late afternoon. Then Grant said that he wanted to go to the Eastern Outlook, the mountain's prize view, facing the Green Mountains of Vermont across the Hudson Valley. He had seen it only once, when he had walked there shortly after arriving at the cottage. Douglas was concerned, but when he asked whether the general felt strong enough for the trip, his patient nodded in reply. The like-

This last photograph of General Grant was taken three days before his death, which occurred on July 23. Harrison Tyrrell, the general's valet, sits in the shadow in the doorway.—Courtesy of Mrs. Lee Gwynne Martin

lihood is that he didn't care: he was bored to extinction. The Bath chair was brought out, and Harrison took the handle. The route chosen was a shortcut, downhill and over a winding path. Harrison, with Colonel Grant, Douglas, and others following, moved at a smart, jolting pace. The general was in no condition to enjoy the view when he got to the Outlook, and, letting Harrison rest a moment, he signaled to go back. On the way back the road was followed. It was uphill over rough ground, and several pairs of hands pushed. They had to cross the railroad tracks at the freight platform, and Grant had to dismount and

One of the last photographs of the general at the Drexel cottage, showing from left to right Drs. Shrady and Douglas (both standing), Mrs. Newman, Mrs. Grant, and General Grant. The seated figure in the background is probably the Reverend Dr. John P. Newman, a fashionable Methodist minister who had been pastor of the Metropolitan Church in Washington during Grant's administration.— Courtesy of The Rutherford B. Hayes Library, Fremont, Ohio

climb some steps while the chair was hoisted up. When he got to the cottage he was badly exhausted. The trip should not have been made, Douglas told reporters late in the evening, "but we were all at fault for allowing it." [60]

The general had eight hours of sleep that night, and the next morning, July 21, passed so quietly that he was thought to be resting and recuperating. But by noon Douglas became concerned that "the dozing quietude of his patient was more that of extreme and growing lassitude than of restful repose." While Douglas was at lunch the family noticed increasing weakness and vagueness on the general's part, and sent for him. Grant told him that he could not endure his weakness much longer, and asked for morphine. Douglas reluctantly gave him a diluted injection, and the general seemed to sleep. That night Douglas reported that his patient was in such critical condition that "he would hazard no prediction of the future, not even of the night." Colonel Grant was believed to have said that he did not think his father would survive the night.[61] That sultry evening Grant's invalid chairs were moved into the parlor, where the air was better. All the family, with Dr. Newman, were gathered around, but at 11:30 Grant whispered to Douglas to tell them all to go to bed. Most of them did so. Ulysses, Jr., who was in New York, had been summoned, and Douglas told reporters at 1:00 in the morning that he had given the general a brandy injection, trying to tide him over until his son arrived.[62]

Douglas, convinced that the end was coming at last, had sent telegrams to Sands and Shrady. They arrived by special train the next afternoon, along with Ulysses, Jr., and his wife. Grant recognized them and shook hands. After a superficial examination they reported "critical weakness," but would predict nothing. Dr. Shrady took charge and, as the general's breath and pulse quickened, "Hypodermics of brandy were given." Early in the evening Colonel Grant asked his father if he would not like to lie down. The general nodded, and Fred and the nurse put him to bed. This was a temporary bed, brought down from the hotel and placed in the parlor, where it still stands. The doctors agreed to continue "the stimulating treatment. The General did not need an anodyne." It was thought that at most he might live until 4:00 in the morning.[63]

As day came, bringing but slight change, it was hoped that the general would last until midday. Dr. Douglas urged the family to get a little rest and most of them retired. The reporters, who had been spending the night in the shadows of a nearby clump of trees, watching the whole scene through the open doors and windows, withdrew to a respectful distance. At 7:00, as he was on the porch for a little air, Henry, the nurse, rushed out and told Douglas that the general was going. Harrison went upstairs and knocked on all the doors, and all converged again around the bed. Just after 8:00 the end came. "There was no expiring sigh," Douglas recalled later. "Life passed away so

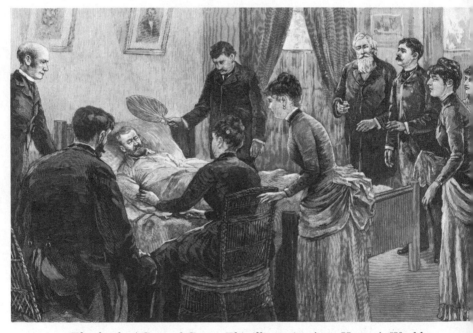

The death of General Grant. This illustration from Harper's Weekly, *August 1, 1885, shows the general as he appeared with his family and physicians early on the morning of July 23.—Courtesy of The New-York Historical Society, New York City*

quietly, so peacefully, that, to be sure it had terminated we waited a minute." The time was 8:08 on the morning of July 23, and Colonel Fred stopped the clock.[64]

Mark Twain got the news by telegraph within an hour or two. In a memorandum jotted down the same morning, he recalled his last visit to the general. "I then believed," he said, "he would live several months. He was still adding little perfecting details to his book. . . . He was through a few days later. Since then the lack of any strong interest to employ his mind has enabled the tedious weariness to kill him. I think his book kept him alive several months. He was a very great man and superlatively good." [65]

Eastern Outlook

5. The General Leaves the Mountain

COLONEL GRANT, exhausted by long vigils, was ably and tactfully assisted in the many arrangements that had to be made following his father's death by W. J. Arkell, whose cottage was only a short distance away. Within half an hour of the general's death, the waiting engine at the mountain depot was on the way to Saratoga to bring Holmes, the local undertaker. Undertaker Stephen J. Merritt of New York had also been summoned. Karl Gerhardt, Mark Twain's protégé sculptor, had been at the hotel for some time, making a study for a proposed statue of Grant. He was called to the cottage at Dr. Newman's suggestion, and prepared a death mask. Augustus Saint-Gaudens, probably the nation's most distinguished sculptor, commissioned by the Century Company, wired for permission to come and make a death mask, but found that he had been forestalled. Gerhardt's mask shortly showed up in the office of Charles L. Webster & Co., who, it was reported, were planning to use it in the preparation of an engraved portrait. The doctors, who were sensitive about some misrepresentations that had been made of their diagnosis, urged an autopsy. The family firmly declined, declaring that they were perfectly satisfied with diagnosis and treatment from beginning to end.[1]

Holmes arrived on a special train, bringing an ice coffin, and the general's body was placed in it. The body was found to be greatly emaciated, and was estimated to weigh less than 100 pounds. Merritt and his son arrived late in the afternoon, bringing with them a set of embalming implements. The work of embalming began at once and was expected to continue all night. Actually, it took longer, and was continued the following night. The ice coffin was so constructed that its sides could be let down to facilitate the work. When the embalming was finished, the ice was no longer needed, but the body was kept in the box until the coffin should arrive. Over it was hung a canopy of broadcloth and satin, resting upon four pillars.[2]

On the evening of the general's death a detachment of G.A.R. veterans from Wheeler Post No. 92, in Saratoga, arrived, pitched a tent between the cottage and the hotel, and went on guard. It was this same organization that had turned out to honor the general when he passed through Saratoga in June. "There is perhaps no occasion for their presence," the *World* observed, "but there is a touching fitness in their loyal devotion to an old leader to which no man can be insensible." The U. S. Grant Post of the G.A.R., a Brooklyn unit, also urged their services as guards, and Colonel Grant, who evidently felt that it would be undiplomatic to decline, accepted them. The Brooklyn contingent arrived the next evening; another tent went up, and arrangements were made for dividing duties. The Brooklyn post was to guard the porch and the room where the general lay; the Saratoga post was to continue guarding the grounds.[3]

The choice of a final resting-place for the general came under discussion almost immediately. Colonel Grant sent many telegrams announcing the death of his father. One went to Mayor W. R. Grace of New York City. The mayor called a meeting of the board of aldermen, and a burial place in one of the city's parks was offered. In notes to Colonel Fred the general had mentioned West Point, Galena, and New York City as possible burial places, adding that he wanted Julia to rest by him eventually and that this would not be permitted at West Point. The prompt offer from the city brought immediate response from Colonel Grant, who asked that someone be sent to confer with him. Chief Clerk W. L. Turner, by direction of the mayor, left for Mount McGregor the same evening.[4]

When Turner arrived the next morning and suggested Riverside Park, he found the Grants opposed. "The family would not
consider it. Central Park seemed to them the proper place."
Telegrams went back and forth, and on July 27 Colonel Grant,
with his brother Jesse and General Horace Porter, went down
to the city to choose a site. Mayor Grace and park officials accompanied them on a tour of the parks, and Colonel Grant was
impressed by the commanding site in Riverside Park that was
shown him last, saying that he would describe its advantages to
his mother. On the next day, after he had returned to Mount
McGregor, he telegraphed Mayor Grace: "Mother takes Riverside Park. Temporary tomb had better be at the same place."
The city officials had all favored this high bluff overlooking the
Hudson River, and pointed out that it was an ideal place for
the monumental tomb that was now in contemplation. There
had been proposals from Washington urging that interment
should properly be there, but Adjutant General R. C. Drum,
who had been at Mount McGregor conferring with the family,
said on his return that he was satisfied with their choice of New
York City.[5]

Other planning went on at the same time. Representatives of
the president and of the governor of New York, as well as of
the mayor, had arrived at Mount McGregor and conferred with
Colonel Grant. Even while Central Park was still the family's
choice as a burial place, it was agreed that the body would lie
at the cottage in the death room until August 4, when funeral
services would be held there. The body would then be taken to
Saratoga, with only a brief pause there to change trains, and
then on to Albany. There it would lie in state in the Capitol
until noon the next day, after which the funeral train would
take it to New York. There the body was to lie in state until
August 8, when there would be public services at the interment
site.[6]

Messages of sympathy to Mrs. Grant and her family began
arriving in great numbers almost at once; the telegraph instruments at the Hotel Balmoral were burdened with outgoing and
incoming messages, to and from official and private sources all

On the evening of Grant's death a detachment of Saratoga Springs Civil War veterans from the Wheeler Post, G.A.R., arrived to patrol the grounds about the cottage, which can be seen in the background, where the general died. This illustration appeared in Harper's Weekly, *August 1, 1885.—Courtesy of The New-York Historical Society, New York City*

over the nation and the world. Resolutions of regret from legisla-
tures in Southern states, and editorials of sympathy prepared for
Southern newspapers, were especially noted. The Charleston
News and Courier editorialized about Grant:

> Happy he was in one sense at the time of his death;
> had his life ended but a few years since the
> mourning for the great leader would have been
> more or less sectional in its manifestations. Dying
> as he now dies, the grief is as widespread as the
> Union, and the sorrow is as National as his
> fame. . . . The good will of all, whether hereto-
> fore friends or not, was his in his agony and will
> abide with his name forever.[7]

"It can be truly said that all the nation mourned," says Mark
Twain's biographer. "General Grant had no enemies, political
or sectional, in those last days. The old soldier battling with a
deadly disease yet bravely completing his task, was a figure at
once so pathetic and so noble that no breath of animosity remained to utter a single word that was not kind." President
Cleveland issued a proclamation announcing Grant's death and
sent a message of sympathy to Julia. There were memorial
services everywhere as messages and carloads of flowers arrived at Mount McGregor.[8]

The body lay in the parlor near the spot where the general
spent his last night, the face peaceful and unclouded by any
trace of suffering, said the *New York Times*. Temporarily, a
flag was furled over the body. "On the breast reposed a wreath
of oak leaves, gathered yesterday by Julia, the Colonel's daughter, and the two child daughters of Dr. Douglas." The three
girls had gone into the woods to search for the leaves, and
Henry, the nurse, had helped them to fashion the wreath.[9] This
oak wreath, later varnished at Colonel Grant's direction, went all
the way to the temporary tomb with the general, and was still
intact when the body was removed to the great mausoleum
nearby, years later.

The flood of sympathy was slow in ebbing. "Letters and messages of condolence and sympathy are still being flashed over the wires and come by mail from everywhere each moment of the day and night," the *New York Tribune* reporter noted two days after the general's death. "These interfere seriously with the sending of dispatches for the press," he stated his personal grievance. After the messages were copied in the telegraph office they were sent at once to Colonel Grant, who read them to his mother. "Such a flood of world-wide sympathy has probably never before been told by the electric spark to suffering hearts, and the family is profoundly grateful." Colonel Grant, swamped with mail, finally gave out a general statement to the effect that much of it could not be opened until after the funeral. It was his desire that all should bear with any delay of correspondence because of the physical impossibility of attending to it at once. "In due time it will be a part of Colonel Grant's pleasure to acknowledge the tokens and tributes to his father." [10]

Mrs. Grant spent most of her time in seclusion, upstairs in the darkened cottage. Her son Fred was her contact point with the outside world. He let few visitors approach her. Mr. Drexel and Mr. Arkell both called on the day of the general's death, and Mr. Drexel "delivered his condolences to Mrs. Grant and the family." Drs. Douglas and Shrady, after resting at the hotel a few hours, returned to the cottage in the afternoon. Grant had come to look upon them almost as brothers. These, with Dr. Newman, were all the visitors that day. Adjutant General Drum came on the following day, bearing President Cleveland's message to Julia and placing the facilities of the government at her disposal. He delivered it to her personally. General Joseph B. Carr, New York secretary of state, a personal friend, was permitted to see the general's face. Senor Romero, the Mexican minister, spent much of July 24 with the family at the cottage. [11]

Saratoga, where the high social season was in full swing, had suddenly been plunged into mourning. When it was learned that Grant's body was to be kept at Mount McGregor until August 4, and would then be transferred through Saratoga without a stop, there was resentment and formal protest. A committee of prominent citizens was formed and went to Mount McGregor, "but were unable to make any arrangement whatever." The *New York Herald* reporter saw a money-making scheme afoot. This was a time that brought human nature to the surface, he commented. "The visit and death of General Grant means a fortune to Mount McGregor, but to Saratoga it means ten days sliced from the very tenderloin of its season." Drexel and Arkell had cared for the Grant family well and naturally expected something in return. "This is the inside spring of the ten days' tarry idea." There were 25,000 people in Saratoga, he pointed out the next day, "every one of whom would be glad to pay a meed of respect to Grant"; but they could not, because of the limited capacity of the little railroad. The body was kept at Mount McGregor, he charged, "Simply to oblige Mr. Drexel, who owns the cottage in which the great General died, and the railroad people and the hotel. Saratoga is in arms and indignant to a degree." Drexel must have been highly indignant, for quite other reasons, and evidently straightened the *Herald* man out on a few facts. At any rate, on the following day there was a partial apology in the newspaper. "Mr. Drexel's hospitality and liberality have been fully and generously taxed," the *Herald* said, announcing that it was setting right some misapprehensions, "and the personal expense of supporting General Grant and all his family with every conceivable consideration is estimated at $1,000 a week. His princely generosity hasn't a taint or suspicion of ostentation about it." Nevertheless, whether it was intentional or not, "the tendency here is to advertise a new resort. The Drexel cottage doesn't belong to Mr. Drexel. It is part of the property owned by a corporation which owns the mountain, the hotel and the pretty little railway between this point and Saratoga." Mr. Arkell received no absolution from the *Herald*.[12]

That Arkell had persuaded the Grant family to keep the general's body on Mount McGregor against their wishes is incredible. The plan fitted it with notes that Grant had left behind, and it was only human that Julia should wish to be left alone with her dead for a time. Time was needed to build the temporary brick tomb in Riverside Park, and meanwhile the body had to be kept somewhere. Nevertheless, the long delay on the

*Colonel Fred Grant's daughter and Dr. Douglas's two daughters
with the aid of Henry McQueeney, Grant's male nurse, made a
wreath of oak which was later varnished, and placed with Grant in
the temporary tomb in Riverside Park, New York City. It was still
intact years later when Grant was moved to the nearby mausoleum
where he lies to this day. This illustration showing the children
placing the wreath is from* Harper's Weekly, *August 8, 1885.—
Courtesy of The New-York Historical Society, New York City*

mountaintop did harmonize with Arkell's hopes for the resort there. The day after the general's death he had announced to the press that he would vacate his own cottage at Artists' Lake, near the hotel, and that "the body will be placed there, the cottage to be sealed, and guarded by the platoon which will be sent by General Hancock." The public would be kept at a distance, "in accordance with the General's desire, expressed a week ago." When all arrangements had been made and a burial place had been chosen, the body would be taken by special train to Albany, and "From Albany the body will be taken by special train to New York, and possibly to Washington, depending upon which city is chosen for the burial." [13] The decision to keep the body at the Drexel cottage instead could only have been made by the family.

July 26 was Sunday, and many visitors came to Mount McGregor. While a Sunday outing on the mountain offered many attractions, they "seemed to be impressed with nothing save the cottage in which the General's body rests." They did not have to ask where it was. There were three large tents at the side and rear of the house; the steady tramp of uniformed sentinels carrying polished muskets, and pieces of crepe hanging upon the doors, told them. Scarcely any of them went away "without plucking a sprig of fern, or blossoming wild flowers which grew near the path that the General used to take when walking or riding in his invalid carriage, and stowing it carefully away in a book or a paper as if it were of priceless value." [14]

As plans for the funeral took form, Manager Fonda of the narrow-gage railroad gave directions for the preparation of a car to take the general's body down the mountain. The railroad's observation car was chosen. This car was 35 feet long and had open sides, with a roof supported by posts. The lengthwise seats were removed from the rear, leaving the car entirely open at that end, where the coffin was to be placed. Seats were left at the front for the guard of honor. The whole car was draped in mourning.[15] The Grant family obviously did not want elaborate ceremony at Mount McGregor, though they did ask for a military funeral in New York, but they had to make concessions to others. The president had placed Major General Winfield S. Hancock, then commanding at Governor's Island, in charge of arrangements for the government's part in the funeral, and Hancock was determined to do full honor to his former chief. Plans for the final ceremony in New York were elaborate, even gigantic, but Hancock was not to be ignored at Mount McGregor either. He sent Colonel Roger Jones, the inspector general, there as his representative, and regular troops began to arrive soon after, to supplement and in part relieve the G.A.R. guard. Company E, 12th Infantry, came from Fort Niagara, and went into camp near the Eastern Outlook. They took over the outside guard at the cottage. Hancock sent word that a battery of artillery was on the way to fire salutes on the day of the funeral. A day or two later the men of Battery A, 5th Artillery, came in from Governor's Island, but without their guns. Finally there arrived Battery B, 4th Artillery, from Fort Adams, Newport, followed on a special train from Saratoga by their four 10-pounder guns and ammunition. They made preparation not only for firing salutes on the day of the funeral service, but also on the arrival of General Hancock. Another battery was sent to Saratoga to fire minute guns as the funeral train passed through that place.[16]

The coffin was specially built. It was of polished oak, lined with copper, covered with dark purple velvet, and had full-length solid silver handles and a nameplate of gold, engraved simply, "U. S. Grant." It arrived in its heavy oak case on July 29. The general's body was removed from the ice coffin and placed in it. Henry and Harrison assisted the undertakers. The body was dressed in a suit of black broadcloth, the coat of the Prince Albert cut. There was a white linen standing collar, and a black silk scarf was tied in a plain bow at the throat. Patent leather slippers were placed upon the dead general's feet over white stockings. There were gold studs in the shirt front and plain gold buttons in the cuffs. The right hand was folded across the breast and the left disposed at the side. Colonel Grant placed on his father's finger a plain gold ring, and put a small packet of mementos in the breast pocket of the coat. The heavy plate-glass inner top of the coffin was dropped in place and sealed by "the turning down of sixty screws that press the glass down into its fittings and which thus render the coffin air-tight." The flag-covered coffin lay in the shadow of the canopy, which was lighted by "an incandescent lamp." In the room G.A.R. veterans of the Brooklyn post were on watch, while members of the Saratoga post kept vigil on the veranda and the outside picket posts were manned by regulars.[17]

There was no uniform to dress the general in, and no sword to lay upon the coffin. All the general's military effects had been turned over to the government, under the agreement with W. H. Vanderbilt, and were by that time housed in the Smithsonian Institution. There was some disappointment expressed over this when the body was put on view, but the Grant family accepted the situation and made no request for the return of a uniform and sword.[18]

The next morning Mrs. Grant came down, accompanied by her son Colonel Fred, and saw the body, while the G.A.R. guards withdrew. It was said to be the first time she had been out of her room upstairs for a week. That afternoon at two o'clock the parlor was opened to the guests at the hotel, who had shown an unobstrusive sympathy that the Grant family appreciated. It was not desired to attract a large crowd that would swamp the cottage, and only a modest notice had been posted. The face of the general was seen beneath the plate glass. "But the light was not good, the face was shadowed, and some thought that discoloration had begun." The news went quickly to Saratoga that the body was on view and the next train was loaded with visitors. They were permitted to see the general's face, although this had not been the original intention.[19]

The embalmers, much exercised by criticisms of their work, applied a bleaching lotion to the general's face next morning, and the body was placed on display again that afternoon. The family had said that the general's body would not be exposed to all, as it had been the day before, but that applications to see it would not be refused. This limited restriction was respected, and it was not until afternoon that a trainload of visitors came from Saratoga, marched in a body to the cottage, and were admitted.[20]

The cottage was closed to the public the following day, but it was stated that this had nothing to do with the embalming. The family felt that they were entitled to a little privacy, and there was little time left for it. Dr. Douglas was, however, summoned by the embalmers to witness their handiwork, and when Mrs. Grant was led to the parlor that afternoon she seemed to have noticed nothing amiss. The embalmers tried to induce Colonel Grant to let visitors in later, "pleading that their exclusion might be misconstrued," but he refused firmly. "He said that the family were satisfied with the body and that should be enough for the embalmers." [21]

There was a thunderstorm on Mount McGregor late in the sultry day of July 30. Electric lights had been installed throughout the hotel and in the cottage at the beginning of the month. Lights had been placed also in the covered way that ran from the hotel down to the railroad station. It was just at dinner time that a bolt of lightning struck the hotel and passed down the wires to the station and the cottage. The wire to the station was not grounded, and two army officers, who had finished dinner and gone down there to inspect the funeral car, were knocked senseless and at first thought killed. The bolt knocked out the light in the cottage parlor and dazed the G.A.R. guard posted there. There was panic at the hotel, where the three telegraph instruments in the lobby were put temporarily out of commission, and there was alarm about what might have happened at the cottage. There was a rush in that direction, but Colonel Fred and Jesse Grant soon left the cottage to go to the hotel for dinner. They told reporters only that the light in the parlor had been burned out and that there had been very minor damage to the nursery room. Later it was found that damage to the nursery room had been fairly extensive; a good bit of plaster had been knocked down and a hole made in the floor. The little son of Colonel Fred was walking across the floor, but "the child was not harmed." The nursemaid went into hysterics, which were not quieted until late in the night. A defective lightning rod, from which a relic hunter had cut a section, was blamed for the damage at the cottage.[22]

Relic hunters were becoming a pest. For the most part, visitors to the mountain were well behaved, but the American penchant for picking up souvenirs soon manifested itself in more objectionable form than the picking of flowers to press in a book. "The passion for relics connected with General Grant is so great," the *World* noted on August 1, "that the funeral car which stood here yesterday had to be removed this morning to the station of the Mount McGregor Railway in Saratoga, where it was placed under lock and key." While it had been guarded by two soldiers, relic hunters had seriously injured its ornaments and even cut out a large piece of the car itself. At the hotel, where the ladies were making mourning rosettes to be used in trimming the car, "Every speck of black cloth which was trimmed off from these rosettes was eagerly picked up by the visitors and carried off." "The relic-hunters would cut the cottage all to pieces inside of a week, and not leave a stick or stone of it standing if the property should be left unprotected," said *Leslie's*.[23]

Another fine Sunday came, and with it trainloads of visitors, some of whom had hoped to get into the Grant cottage but most of whom were content to walk by or gather on a nearby knoll. The family remained in seclusion, except that in the afternoon they were joined by the Reverend Dr. Newman and Mrs. Newman for devotional services. In the rear of the cottage, screened from public view, the veteran Willett amused the children. He had constituted himself the children's playman and protector. There were still three of them at the cottage: "Colonel Fred's little boy, aged four, named after his grandfather; Julia, his sister, nine, pretty and demure; Nellie, Jesse Grant's little girl, a bright, pretty child of three." The old soldier, who had served three years under Grant, had become quite expert in the handling of the children. He had rigged up for them swings and a croquet ground, and a summerhouse thatched with boughs and leaves, "and there they play every day." [24]

The next day, August 3, General Hancock arrived with his staff on the ten o'clock train. The battery posted near the East-

The funeral of General Grant. Top left, regulars on guard at Mount McGregor; top right, Hotel Balmoral and surrounding buildings with Drexel Cottage left center; center, funeral train descending the mountain; bottom, temporary tomb in Riverside Park. Views from Frank Leslie's Illustrated Newspaper, *August 8, 1885.— Courtesy of General Research and Humanities Division; The New York Public Library; Astor, Lenox and Tilden Foundations*

ern Outlook was prepared to fire a salute in his honor, but when Colonel Jones went aboard the train to meet Hancock, the general had the good taste to stop it. The other two companies of regulars were lined up in full dress on the cottage side of the railway tracks, and presented arms as he proceeded to the cottage. With him were General Rufus Ingalls, once Grant's roommate at West Point, and other officers. Colonel Grant presented them to Mrs. Grant and the family, they passed through the parlor, viewing the body, and then went up to the hotel. They soon returned to Saratoga, where Hancock was the guest of Mr. Drexel, and their departure was the signal for the guard at the cottage to open the parlor to visitors. A heavy and persistent rain, however, beginning in midafternoon, practically put an end to the respectful parade from the little railroad station.[25]

On the eve of the funeral, as final plans were reviewed, it became doubtful that Mrs. Grant would leave the cottage. Following the funeral train at three o'clock the same afternoon, a special train was to take the ladies of the Grant family to Saratoga, "with the possible exception of Mrs. Grant." She had been debating all day the advisability of going to New York. The family wanted her to go, but her objection was "that what she would see there could only wound her sorrow, while it would have no compensating comfort." Mrs. Newman, it was said, would be her companion whether she went or stayed. Colonel Fred's wife, Ida, was a sister of Mrs. Potter Palmer of Chicago. Mr. and Mrs. Palmer were at Mount McGregor, and they and Mr. Arkell were to accompany the ladies going to New York.[26]

The day of the funeral arrived with heavy overcast following an all-night rain, and a 13-gun salute fired at dawn was muffled. It cleared to an almost perfect day about eight o'clock, and the half-hourly salutes thereafter were clearly heard. Visitors began arriving early, by farm wagon, buggy, stage, and carriage. Trains ran as fast as the mountain engine could pull them, each train loaded to capacity. At 9:30 the cottage was opened to visitors, and they filed through the parlor in a steady line for half an hour. The Reverend Dr. Newman led a party of clergymen to the cottage, and seats were then provided for them in front of the eastern porch. Visitors gathered behind them. General Hancock arrived in a special train with his staff, accompanied by General William T. Sherman, Admiral Stephen C. Rowan, Senators Warner Miller and William M. Evarts, ex-Secretary of State Hamilton Fish, Joseph W. Drexel and his family, and ex-Congressman Thomas P. Ochiltree of Texas. Colonel Jones escorted them past the two companies of regulars, drawn up by the station, to the porch, where Colonel Grant led them to chairs on the side porch. The troops followed and formed a line facing the cottage about 50 feet away.

Then from all sides the people drew in toward the cottage. Way was made for General Porter, for ex-Postmaster General John A. J. Creswell and Mrs. Creswell, for Mr. and Mrs. Arkell, and for Senor Romero. Seats were provided for them back of General Hancock's party. The parlor was given up to the immediate family, while General Ingalls and relatives of the general and Mrs. Grant occupied other rooms on the lower floor. On the porch between the parlor door and the corner there was a small stand covered with a black-bordered flag, on which a Bible rested. Dr. Newman's chair was close to it. With him were Methodist Episcopal Bishop W. L. Harris of New York, the Reverend Dr. Benjamin L. Agnew of Philadelphia, and Dr. Douglas. Members of the honor guard were also seated on the porch. On the steps sat Comrade Henry Camp of the Brooklyn G.A.R. post, who was to lead the singing, with a small group to assist him.[27]

The services beginning at ten o'clock were simple. Dr. Agnew read the 90th Psalm. Then Bishop Harris prayed, and all joined in the Lord's Prayer. Mr. Camp signaled his assistants, a group of singers from Boston, Brooklyn, and New York, who joined him on the porch and led the assembly in the hymn, "My Faith Looks Up to Thee." Dr. Newman delivered the funeral address, reading from a manuscript for one hour and twenty-five minutes, on the text, "Well done, thou good and faithful servant, enter thou into the joy of thy Lord." He reviewed Grant's entire career in highly eulogistic terms, comparing him to Washington in public life, praising his private life, and insisting that the general was a man of prayer. The service closed about noon with the singing of "Nearer, my God, to Thee," and the benediction by Bishop Harris.

The family then withdrew, and many on the porch went into the parlor. Others tried to enter, and a guard was placed on the porch. After some delay the coffin was closed. A guard of honor from the Brooklyn post carried the coffin. Troops with reversed arms led the way, with bugles sounding a dirge. Then came the clergymen and Dr. Douglas, the three Grant boys and General Sherman, and the Brooklyn guard with the coffin. A guard from the Loyal Legion, of which Grant had been New York State commander, followed, and then came General Hancock and his staff and party. They followed the path to the station, and the funeral train started for Saratoga just after the guns at the Outlook had fired the one o'clock salute. The battery remained to fire a 38-gun salute at sunset. While the funeral train was en route from the mountain to Saratoga, the casket was opened by order of General Hancock, "and the guard of Wheeler post were accorded the privilege of taking their last look at the remains of the illustrious dead." [28]

The transfer of the coffin to the main line was made at Saratoga with only a brief pause. The coffin was carried in procession to the Capitol at Albany, and the general lay in state there until the next noon. The funeral train then proceeded to New York, passing respectful crowds all the way. In the city the coffin was placed in City Hall, where during the next two days nearly 250,000 people filed past and viewed the body. On August 8 the immense funeral procession marched all the way from City Hall to Riverside Park, where the coffin, encased in further metal covering, was placed in the temporary brick tomb. "Such a mighty outpouring of people in the streets," the *New York Tribune* recorded, "such a marshalling of men in one array the inhabitants of New-York never saw." [29]

Julia had decided not to leave Mount McGregor, but General Sherman sent her a message telling her that "such a funeral never before occurred in America and never will again." He added a graceful tribute that touched her heart:

On August 8 there was an immense funeral procession for Grant which marched all the way from City Hall to Riverside Park, where the body was placed in the temporary tomb. This illustration showing Major General Hancock and his staff leading the march appeared in Harper's Weekly, *August 15, 1885.—Courtesy of The New-York Historical Society, New York City*

May you continue for many years to receive tokens of love and affection and then rest at that majestic spot on the Banks of the Hudson made sacred by the presence of the mortal part of the Great and Good General, to whom you were as true as the needle to the thread, in poverty as in health, in adversity as well as in exaltation.[30]

Colonel Grant had to return to Mount McGregor almost at once. His mother needed comfort, to be sure, but he also had an immense amount of unfinished business to attend to. There were endless acknowledgments to be made, and there were the proofs of the second volume of his father's book to review and revise. The papers and memoranda were in the office room at the cottage, where they had been locked when the general began to sink. Dawson, the stenographer, went with him. The colonel, with his wife and children and Mrs. Sartoris, left New York on August 10. Also in his party were Mr. and Mrs. Arkell, returning to their cottage on the mountain, and Dr. and Mrs. Douglas, whose children were still at the hotel there.[31]

Mr. Childs reported from Long Branch that Mrs. Grant had decided to remain the guest of Mr. Drexel at Mount McGregor until October 1. What she would do after that had not been determined. It was expected that she would give up the house on East 66th Street, which was still in her name, and take a smaller house. Mr. Childs had expected that Mrs. Grant and Mrs. Sartoris would be the guests of Mrs. Childs at Long Branch. "Mrs. Grant was desirous of coming for a change of scene and the sea air, but concluded finally that the privacy of the Mount McGregor cottage would be better than the unavoidable publicity of the Branch." Mrs. Sartoris would be returning to her husband's home in England in a few days.[32]

Mr. and Mrs. Potter Palmer visited Mrs. Grant at Mount McGregor later in the month. After their return to their home in Chicago, Mr. Palmer told the press that "Mrs. Grant was feeling quite cheerful—or as cheerful as could possibly be expected. She likes to have a few intimate friends about her now." Mr. Palmer said that Colonel Fred's little daughter was at the Palmer home, and he expected that the colonel and his wife would come there later. Speaking of the financial affairs of the Grant family, he said he hadn't discussed this with them, but he was sure they could not be in much worse shape. "The General's book, though, promised a big return." The family would carry out the general's request "to devote the first proceeds of the book to paying relatives of the Grants who lost money through Ferdinand Ward's rascality." [33]

Mrs. Grant evidently changed her mind about staying at the cottage until October 1, for the *Daily Saratogian* reported her and the family as leaving Mount McGregor for New York City on August 31. No doubt Colonel Grant found that the final work on the second volume of the *Memoirs* could be done more conveniently in the city, where he would be near the publishers, and persuaded his mother to leave with him. Before he left the mountain, he wrote a graceful letter of appreciation to Mr. Drexel for all that the Drexels had done for the general. "The last three weeks of my father's life," he said, "I believe are due to the comfortable change from N. Y. to your cottage. Every thing that could possibly be done for his comfort was done." After a brief stay in a hotel, they reopened the house on East 66th Street. Little Julia in later years remembered her father as being very busy with her grandfather's book for a long time after they returned to the house. [34]

In September Henry Ward Beecher, the famous preacher of Brooklyn, was asked to deliver a eulogy on Grant. He asked Mark Twain for an advance copy of the *Personal Memoirs* to obtain light, especially on Grant's drinking habits. Mark answered that he had promised Webster, who was in Europe, not to give anybody sight or copy of the book; otherwise he would send him one at once. He said that army friends of the general had given him the impression that Grant sometimes went on sprees before he came East to take over the command of all the Union armies, but that he had stopped before accepting the high command. "The only time General Grant ever mentioned liquor to me," Twain told Beecher, "was about last April or possibly May. He said: 'If I could only build up my strength! The doctors urge whisky or champagne, but I can't take them; I can't

abide the taste of any kind of liquor.' Had he made a conquest
so complete that even the *taste* of liquor was become an offense?
Or was he so sore over what had been said about his habit that
he wanted to persuade others and likewise himself that he hadn't
even ever *had* any taste for it? It sounded like the latter, but
that's no evidence." In the fall of 1884, Mark went on, Grant
had conquered not only the habit of smoking cigars but even
the inclination to smoke. He had gone at the root, not the trunk.
Beecher should talk to Generals Sherman and Van Vliet; they
knew all about Grant. Sherman had told Twain on the day of
Grant's funeral that he was made sick by some of the newspaper
nonsense about Grant's purity. It was being said, in the general
chorus of praise after his death, that he had not even enjoyed
bawdy jokes. "Grant was no namby-pamby fool, he was a *man*
—all over—rounded and complete," said Sherman. Twain told
Beecher that he would find not a hint in the book about Grant's
drinking. He was sore on the point. "I wish I had thought of it!
I would have said to General Grant: 'Put the drunkenness in
the Memoirs—and the repentance and reform. Trust the
people.' " [35]

The general had hoped to go over the proofs of the revised
second volume himself, but had finally resigned himself to
having it done by his son. Mark Twain, who was under very
heavy financial pressure, had proposed to Webster after Grant's
death that they bring out both volumes at the same time, on
December 1. Webster knew that this was out of the question,
and seems not to have given serious thought to the suggestion.
It seemed impossible to bring out the first volume alone on time,
as the sale had been greatly stimulated by the general's death.
The publication date was finally met, however, and the sale was
enormous. Twain and Webster, though, had difficulties with
Colonel Fred, who was still tinkering with the proofs of the second volume. Webster in November complained to Mark that the
colonel had removed some of the material from the *Memoirs*
"about Butler being bottled up in the Peninsula"; it was "thrown
away as of no use." He had then sold the material to the *North
American Review,* Webster said. Near the end of December,

with the publication date for the second volume little more than two months away, he told Twain that "I can't do a thing with Col. Grant." He had altered the proof extensively; "I found it so changed and patched that it made me nervous." Webster had reversed Colonel Fred in some of his alterations, and Twain approved his "stet." "It won't *do* to leave things out & make unnecessary alterations in the General's text." He offered to come to the city and give Webster a hand. "I would rather do that, any time, than have the General's work marred. Alterations for the sake of avoiding Badeau's language have gone plenty far enough already—I'm a thundering sight more afraid of the one than of the other." The colonel, evidently, was determined to purify the text of any lingering traces of Badeau's handiwork. Publication of the second volume was delayed two months past schedule.[36] Meanwhile, the profits from the first volume had been spectacular. Webster, with something of a flourish, presented to Mrs. Grant on February 27, 1886, the anniversary of the signing of the book contract, a check for $200,000, the largest royalty check in history. In the end more than 300,000 two-volume sets of Grant's *Personal Memoirs* were sold, and between $420,000 and $450,000 were paid to her. Mark Twain's prophecy had been fulfilled.[37]

The tragic circumstances under which Grant wrote his book, of course, added enormously to its sale, but it has stood on its own merits. When the first volume appeared, the *New York Tribune* gave a full page to the event, quoting extensively and commenting on the style as "a model of simplicity and directness." The author, it said, possessed a literary ability for which the world never gave him credit, "and which he himself probably did not suspect." He had succeeded in describing his personal experiences "without vaunting his services," the "best possible proof of the strength and simplicity of his character." "His *Personal Memoirs* stays alive and is read today," says Bruce Catton, "not simply because it recounts the wartime experiences of a famous soldier but primarily because it is a first-class book—well-written, with a literary quality that keeps it fresh. . . . marked above all by clarity of expression." Edmund

Wilson some years ago, reviewing a reprint edition of Grant's book, became fascinated by the narrative. Grant had, he said, "conveyed—as, so far as I know, no other writer of the period does—the suspense that he and his army, that all those who believed in the Union, felt. The reader becomes absorbed—he is actually on edge to know how the Civil War is coming out." [38]

6. The Cottage Becomes a Shrine

ON THE very day of Grant's death there was discussion of what should be done with the cottage. "It has been proposed that the cottage should be deeded to the Government," the *New York Times* reported, "that a fence should be put around it, and that it be preserved about as the Grant family leave it." This was, of course, pretty much what Mr. Arkell had had in mind in the first place. Mr. Drexel had consented to do this, it was said, if it should seem advisable. There was some bric-a-brac in the cottage that had been taken from his own home. These articles he would remove, "but he would leave the furniture, carpets, and other belongings as they were in the general's lifetime." By the next day Drexel had gone further in his thinking. He authorized a statement "that the cottage will never again be occupied by any family or persons." He would in due time present it to the state or national government, "intact, with all its present belongings, furniture, and fixtures, as a gift to the Nation or Commonwealth." He thought of it as "a museum or a kind of Mount Vernon." He could take care of it himself as long as he lived and might bind his heirs, but he could not feel sure that it would be properly kept. "I hope the public won't regard this cottage idea of mine as an advertisement or show," he told a reporter. "There is no money in it, I assure you." [1]

While planning was going forward for the funeral, and for the monumental mausoleum that was being proposed by leading citizens in New York City, the Mount McGregor promoters had another idea. The directors of the company were mostly on the

117

mountain on August 2, and they talked of leading a popular subscription, after the monument fund should have been completed, "for cutting in the granite face of the hill a colossal profile of the General finishing his book." The figure would be about 30 feet high, cut into the ledge near the Eastern Outlook. At this place it could be seen from trains of the Delaware and Hudson Railroad, passing along the valley about four miles away. The estimated cost was about $100,000, and the figure would, of course, be "a lasting memorial." This project, which anticipated the Mount Rushmore and Stone Mountain memorials by a great many years, probably came from the fertile brain of W. J. Arkell. It was never carried out. The fund for the Grant monument, or Grant's Tomb, as it came to be called, was not completed for a number of years, and by that time the Mount McGregor memorial was forgotten.[2]

Drexel went ahead, however, with the plan to donate the cottage and its contents to the federal government. In the following March a New York congressman, no doubt following his instructions, presented in the House "a bill (H.R. 7338) authorizing the United States to take from Joseph W. Drexel a conveyance of the Grant cottage, located upon Mount McGregor, in the State of New York." The bill was read twice and, without debate, referred to the Committee on Public Buildings and Grounds. The chairman turned the bill over to a hostile subcommittee and, to the indignation of the *Times,* it was never presented on the floor.[3]

The next year Drexel approached the G.A.R., through General Lucius Fairchild, then its national commander. He offered to the Union veterans, in perpetuity, free of expense, "the cottage on Mount McGregor in which Gen. U. S. Grant died." There was no stipulation as to its use, but it was specified that the trustees should include the national commander of the G.A.R., the president of the Mount McGregor railroad, "and such other person as Mr. Drexel or his successor as President of the Drexel & Morgan Banking Company may designate." The offer was referred to the executive committee of the G.A.R. council of administration. Fairchild wrote Drexel that if he could properly accept the trusteeship for himself and his successors he would do so at once, but he did not feel that he had the authority.[4]

At the national encampment of the G.A.R. in September, Fairchild read Drexel's letter and referred the offer to the incoming national commander and council, recommending approval, "if the details of trusteeship and management can be arranged to their entire satisfaction." Acceptance was not immediately forthcoming. The G.A.R. was not created to hold or administer real estate, and the gift needed the approval of the New York State legislature. Mr. Drexel died not long after. There was some doubt that the cottage might not revert to the Drexel estate. The gift had not been found in his will, and his heirs were not bound by the offer. "The failure of the Legislature to act promptly in regard to authorizing the acceptance by

Memorial cartoon from Puck, *July 29, 1885. Japanese admirers of the general reproduced this in colored silk and presented it to Mrs. Grant.—Courtesy of General Research and Humanities Division; The New York Public Library; Astor, Lenox and Tilden Foundations*

the Grand Army of the Republic of the Drexel cottage, in which
Gen. Grant passed his last hours," the *Times* said, was responsible for this situation.[5]

The executors, who were Mrs. Drexel and W. J. Arkell,
proved willing to carry out Mr. Drexel's known wishes, and a
way was found of accomplishing his purpose. A nonprofit association known as the Mount McGregor Memorial Association
was formed, incorporated by the legislature and, on February
19, 1889, accepted transfer of title to the cottage from the executors. The association, which seems to have been pretty much
what Drexel had in mind in his proposal of 1887, included as
corporators William J. Arkell; William Warner, commander in
chief of the Grand Army of the Republic; N. Martin Curtis,
department commander of the Grand Army of the Republic for
the Department of New York; Josiah Porter, adjutant general,
State of New York; and John Kellogg, President of the Saratoga,
Mount McGregor and Lake George Railroad Company. The
successors of Warner, Curtis, Porter, and Kellogg in their respective offices were to succeed them in the corporation. "This
corporation is created," the act of incorporation stated, "for the
purpose of receiving the title to the Drexel cottage on Mount
McGregor, . . . in which the late Ulysses S. Grant passed the
last months of his life and died, and the lot of land on which said
cottage stands, and the contents of said cottage, and of holding
and maintaining the same forever." This was to be a trust in
behalf of the veterans and of the whole American people, and
the public was to be allowed to visit the cottage under reasonable regulations.[6]

This transfer of title was not a gift to either the national or the
state G.A.R. as such, and it did not carry with it any maintenance fund. The New York Department of the G.A.R., feeling
called upon to take the initiative in raising the necessary funds,
asked the national G.A.R. to supply them, and at the 1889 national encampment $1,000 was authorized for the purpose. A
"most worthy and needy comrade was placed in charge of the
property." This was Oliver P. Clarke, of Utica, a Union veteran

whose health had been undermind in the Confederate prison at Andersonville. His friends and physicians had persuaded him to take the position. Clarke entered on duty November 2.[7]

It was found that no means had been provided to heat the cottage or keep it dry. "The walls and furniture were being damaged and destroyed by the frosts of winter and the dampness of spring and fall." An appeal was made to the national commander for funds to install a furnace, but he did not feel authorized to make the expenditure. J. Wesley Smith, "a worthy, generous, patriotic comrade," came to the rescue and bought, paid for and installed a furnace. He received the thanks of the state G.A.R. at its next annual encampment. There were other needs to be met, however. There was no flag for the cottage, the cellar walls were in need of repair, and a cistern or other emergency water supply was needed, the nearest water supply in winter, when the Hotel Balmoral was closed, being some distance from the cottage. Mrs. Clarke recalled later that it took some time to make the place habitable.[8]

In 1891 the state commander of the G.A.R. reported at the annual encampment that he had visited the Grant cottage on Mount McGregor, "and found that comrade O. P. Clarke was carefully protecting the property and valuable relics of our illustrious and beloved commander, Ulysses S. Grant." The national G.A.R. had provided funds for the custodian and some repair, but the national commander felt that "the national government should provide for the maintenance and care of this sacred spot, where the Immortal Chieftain won his greatest victories over disease and death." He had brought the subject to the attention of Congress.[9]

This second appeal to the federal government bore no fruit. Two years later the state commander reported to his comrades that custodian Clarke was doing an excellent job, and "cared for the property as though it were his own." The expense had been borne by the national G.A.R., but at the last meeting of its administrative council it had been voted to discontinue the custodian's salary after April 30, 1893. He therefore appointed a committee to report a plan for the support and maintenance of the cottage, "wholly or in part by the comrades of the State of New York." This was to be a temporary measure, he expected, "believing that an appeal to Congress or to the State of New York is the best thing to do at the proper time." The committee reported in favor of a small head tax on the comrades of the state G.A.R., and the report was approved.[10]

In 1894 the state commander reviewed the history of the movement to preserve the Grant cottage. The national G.A.R. would no longer bear the burden, and efforts to get action from Congress had failed. While the G.A.R. as an organization was not included in the act of incorporation of the Mount McGregor Memorial Association, he said, the general belief was that the association was to stand for and represent the G.A.R., and that organization was "bound morally, if not legally, to maintain the trust which through sentiments of patriotism and honor, was formally accepted in 1889." There seemed no choice for the state organization but to continue the support of the cottage for the time being. If they did not do so, he said, "the door of the Grant cottage may well bear this inscription, 'closed by the Men who Made His Glory.' " A committee had been appointed, however, to make another attempt to interest Congress. "Failing in this, they were to ascertain what the State of New York would do." [11]

The state G.A.R. bore the expense of caring for the Grant cottage again the next year, but the commander urged that some permanent method of support be found. The Wheeler Post No. 92, of Saratoga Springs, now offered to take charge of the Grant cottage for $300 a year. There was doubt of the legality of such an arrangement, since the state G.A.R. had only one member on the board of the Mount McGregor Memorial Association. It was voted instead to continue the head tax on the state comrades for another year, while the incoming council of administration gave further study to the problem.[12]

Relief for the veterans came in 1896. The head tax was no longer providing enough money to pay the custodian's salary, and the state G.A.R. commander had learned that Clarke had to pay for painting and repairs out of the meager sum supplied him. He had therefore called a meeting of the memorial association, he reported to the annual encampment, and, it being "the unanimous opinion that the property was being well cared for," Clarke's appointment was extended for five years. He had then suggested an effort to raise a fund of $25,000 to support the maintenance of the cottage on a permanent basis, but the other trustees of the association wanted to try the State of New York first. He was therefore requested to draft a bill to present to the legislature appropriating the sum of $1,000 annually for the purpose. "I performed this work," the commander reported, and "placed the bills in the hands of Comrade P. H. Murphy, of Post 140, Member of Assembly from New York City, and Senator Edgar T. Brackett, of Saratoga." With some lobbying "by the Comrades of this Department," the measure passed both houses and was then before the governor for signature. The bill was duly signed and became a law on May 14. It amended the act of 1889 by providing for a sum of $1,000 to be paid annually to the Mount McGregor Memorial Association, for the care and maintenance of the Grant cottage.[13] While the act was to be effective immediately, the first appropriation was made only in the following year. An item then appeared in a miscellaneous appropriation act, "To O. P. Clarke for salary as custodian of the Grant cottage situated on Mount McGregor, Saratoga county, for the years eighteen hundred and ninety-six and eighteen hundred and ninety-seven, two thousand dollars. . . ." What Clarke had been living on in the meantime is not clear.[14]

There were plans at this time to extend the Mount McGregor railroad, which had changed hands and undergone foreclosure, to Glens Falls and make it an electric, or interurban trolley, line. The railroad was merged into the Saratoga Northern Railroad for this purpose. Unfortunately, the Hotel Balmoral, the focal point of the whole development, burned in 1897 and the railroad was later abandoned. W. J. Arkell, the chief promoter of the original Mount McGregor development, took a cynical view of this episode. He said in his old age that General Grant's death, contrary to his expectations, "Instead of making the place," had "killed it absolutely. After his death, as people came to the mountain, the moment they stepped off the train they took off their hats and walked around on tiptoes, looking for something I never could find." While the hotel seems to have enjoyed some popularity among summer residents of Saratoga Springs throughout its existence, the hard times of the 1890s no doubt reduced patronage and the mountain development as a whole did not pay off. "Finally I sold the place," Arkell recorded,

Grant's temporary brick tomb. This was in Riverside Park near the site of the present General Grant National Memorial (popularly known as Grant's Tomb), which was not finished until 1897.—Courtesy of The Rutherford B. Hayes Library, Fremont, Ohio

"—the mountain, the hotel and the railroad—for $50,000. Somebody burned the hotel, and the parties who owned it cleared $150,000, and they had the rails and the railroad equipment besides." While he and his family had prospered in other ventures, "we lost another fortune trying to make Mount McGregor a summer resort." [15]

At first O. P. Clarke, as custodian of the Grant cottage on the state payroll, was apparently expected to pay for the upkeep of the place out of his salary, as he had done while the G.A.R. was paying it. But soon separate additional items for maintenance and repair began to appear in the appropriation acts. From 1896 to 1907, inclusive, the State of New York appropriated $15,150 for all purposes at the cottage. The place itself was well cared for, but, as the railroad was abandoned, visitation fell. "When the railroad was running from Saratoga Springs," it was noted in 1908, "from 10,000 to 15,000 persons a year visited the cottage from all parts of the world. During the past year there were about 4,000 visitors." [16]

Clarke carried on under these rather discouraging conditions until his death. The Saratoga Springs guidebook for 1910 still listed Mount McGregor as a local attraction. "On the top of the mountain," it said, "is the Grant cottage, where the great president died. This cottage is preserved by the government as it was when the general breathed his last. In it is the clock which was stopped at the hour when he died, the many gifts which he received before his death, and the furniture of the house as it was at that time." The house was in charge of a caretaker who willingly explained the relics and pointed out the walks that the general took in the days before his death. There were many beautiful views to be had from the mountain, and there were picnicing places and lakes. Clarke's rank had grown with time. "The caretaker of the property," said the guidebook, "is Col. O. P. Clarke, a veteran of the Civil War. The trip may easily be made and the visitor should never fail to take it." [17] The faithful O. P. Clarke passed on in 1917, but his widow Martha took over as custodian and, at the age of 70, began an intensive study of the life of General Ulysses S. Grant. It is recorded of her that she could hold her own in any discussion of the campaigns of the Civil War. She died in 1941. Mrs. A. J. Gambino, who had lived with the Clarkes on Mount McGregor since 1914, then became custodian and is still on duty at the Grant cottage.[18]

As late as 1924, W. J. Arkell, though living in Los Angeles, was still the president of the Mount McGregor Memorial Association, and this organization still held title to the cottage and a small surrounding lot. But the association finally expired, as such memorial groups have a way of doing after the passage of a generation or two. In 1957 the association was formally dissolved by law and the State of New York took title to the Grant cottage. It was provided that "The said premises shall be maintained in their present condition, without change in any respect other than such as may be necessary to so preserve the same, and shall be open to visit by the public without charge, under

General Grant National Memorial, commonly known as Grant's Tomb, Riverside Park, New York City. Inside are the remains of the general and his wife, as well as two trophy rooms containing mural exhibits illustrating Grant's life and military campaigns. This monument was built at a cost of $500,000 over a period of six years and dedicated in 1897.—Courtesy of the National Park Service

reasonable regulations to be prescribed by the education department." [19]

Some years after the hotel burned, the Metropolitan Life Insurance Company bought the largely abandoned mountaintop and built there a sanitarium for its tubercular employees. The first patients arrived in 1913, and facilities for 350 patients, in 20 buildings, were ultimately provided. As the company developed stricter examinations for prospective employees, with annual checkups after employment, there was a steady decrease in tuberculosis among its personnel. Although the sanitarium's facilities were increasingly made available to other types of employee patients, it was decided in 1945 to dispose of this expensive facility. [20]

At this very time Governor Thomas E. Dewey of New York was seeking facilities for the rehabilitation of World War II veterans. Mount McGregor, with the extensive group of hospital buildings there, seemed ideally suited to the purpose. The officers of the Metropolitan Life Insurance Company were delighted with the suggestion; the mountaintop was sold to the State of New York, and the sanitarium was closed. The area came to be known as the Mount McGregor State Veterans Rest Camp, and it cared, on a limited period basis, for "ex-servicemen not ill enough for admission to Veterans Administration hospitals." As its patient load dwindled over the years, Governor W. Averell Harriman, in 1957, proposed that it be converted into a mental hospital. There was loud opposition among veterans' organizations, and Harriman retired in some confusion. The move was delayed for a time. Early in the administration of Governor Nelson A. Rockefeller, however, the change was made and the facilities at Mount McGregor became an annex to the Rome State School for the Mentally Retarded. [21]

The institution later came to be known as the Wilton School. Plans for moving the school down into the valley near the town of Wilton are now far advanced. With the closing of the school on Mount McGregor, the State of New York will have there, with little or no further land acquisition necessary, a splendid site for a small state park combining recreational and historic

values. At present, access to the Grant cottage, which the state
is by law obliged to keep open to the public, can be had only
through the grounds of the school, and visitation is limited. The
removal of the outmoded hospital buildings, the opening of more
direct access, and the improvement of interpretation, would
bring more visitors to the cottage. The accessibility of the dramatic, wooded mountaintop itself, without the presence of the
rather depressing school, should bring many more bent only on
outdoor recreation. Such a project is certainly worth attention.

In the effort to interpret to the public the lives of major figures
in American history, the physical sites available for the purpose
váry widely in number and quality. In the case of General
Ulysses S. Grant there are several houses, many battlefields, and
the imposing tomb on Riverside Drive in New York City. The
State of Ohio maintains his humble birthplace on the Ohio
River, private persons in Missouri care for the log house that he
built with his own hands, the State of Illinois keeps the house
in Galena where he lived briefly after the Civil War, the Na-

*Mosaic depicting the meeting of Grant and Lee at Appomattox,
north vault of the General Grant National Memorial.—Courtesy
of the National Park Service*

tional Park Service provides for the battlefields where he won fame and for the tomb where he and his beloved Julia rest. The tragic but triumphant climax of Grant's career, nevertheless, is indissolubly associated with the plain cottage on Mount Mc-Gregor. Here he fought off death long enough to complete his immortal *Personal Memoirs,* in an agony and an effort watched by all the world. The site is worthy of more attention than it has received in recent years from the State of New York.

Drexel Cottage, from Century Magazine, *July 1908.—*
Courtesy of General Research and Humanities Division;
The New York Public Library; Astor, Lenox and Tilden
Foundations

Appendix
Notes
Bibliographical Note
Index

Appendix
The Death of General Grant

"Records of the Last Days of the Magnanimous Soldier U. S. Grant,"
pp. 277–85, John Hancock Douglas Papers, Library of Congress

July 20. Monday.

. . . During the morning after he had taken his breakfast, he
went out on the piazza, the day being a very good one, temperature on the piazza 68°, with a tendency upward. . . .

I had become very apprehensive, and had been so for several
days. The reporters were asking me if it was safe for them to go
to Saratoga. I replied that I thought sufficient warning would be
given, but should advise them not to absent themselves for any
time from the mountain.

When consulted about one of the family going to Saratoga on
a short visit, I advised against it. Everything looked as favorable
as it had, and the General's own statement confirmed the impression that no immediate and serious change was imminent,
still I noticed in a way hardly to be explained, that the end was
drawing near.

At 4 P.M. this day, he wrote me: "What do you think of my
taking the Bath wagon, and going to overlook the South view?"
(Eastern outlook).

I called for Col. Grant, and told him his father's request, and
asked the General if he felt strong enough to take the ride; to
which he nodded his head affirmatively.

Harrison was called, and with the Colonel we started down
the hill, passed the station, making a stop where the first good

view of the plain is obtained, when a halt was made for an instant.

Then we went on to the summer-house of the Eastern outlook, where another halt was made. It was now a question whether we should return the way we came down, or make the tour which would lead us up the hill, and as we supposed, back to the cottage, another way. The ascent was quite steep, and at its summit the road terminated at a platform used by the Railroad for dumping coal, upon the opposite side of which the road commenced again.

I had never been around this road, nor had Col. Grant. We both thought the road was continuous, and that all we had to do was to drag the chair up, which would fatigue only those who pulled.

Arrived at the summit, we found that the chair had not only to be lifted over the track, but on to the platform over some coal lying there. This could not be easily done, while the General was seated in it, so he alighted from the chair, mounted the platform by three steps, picked his way through the coal, and stood there a moment, while the Bath chair was lifted up, when he again entered the chair, and was drawn to the cottage.

On the way back, we passed under the covered way which led to the hotel. Just as we crossed the plank path of this covered way, we met some ladies coming from the hotel, who saluted the General. He responded by lifting his hat.

I noticed that he was very pale. We hurried him to the side of the cottage, where the steps were few. He walked up with the Colonel's aid, and when he entered his own room, sank immediately into his chair, from which he did not again stir that night.

July 21. Tuesday.

The night passed with a quietness which we supposed was sleep, so that when morning came, we thought he had had eight hours of at least restful repose. The pulse was not any more frequent, but it had not gained in volume.

As this day advanced, what with the steadily increasing heat, the thermometer registering 85°, sultry and stifling, the inability to take food, the return of the attacks of hiccough, and the increasing restlessness, it became very apparent that the General was not regaining the strength he had yesterday morning. Liquid food was presented to him frequently. He would try to swallow it, but after taking a mouthful or two, it would induce coughing, and be rejected.

The amount of food taken today has been very small. Alcoholic stimulants he persistently declines.

The weakness is evidently increasing. I could not yield to his request to give him a large hypodermic injection of morphine, for fear that in his weakened condition it would submerge him by its narcotic effect.

Two or three minute doses were given for its stimulating effect, and to satisfy the demand of the patient. Several times he rose from his chair, and stepped over to the cot near by, upon which he rested for a moment, while the pillows in his chair were being refreshed and then back again to the chair.

As night came on, he seemed to revive for a moment, and again tried to take food, but the effort was practically in vain, the amount swallowed not materially relieving the sense of weakness.

Toward the close of the afternoon, the General came into the parlor, where he sat only a few moments, when he arose, and by Mrs. Grant's aid, returned to his own room, where the feeling of weakness suddenly coming over him, he sank languidly into his chair, letting his cane fall from his hand.

Henry was by his side, having followed him in.

The pillows in the chair upon which he sat needing re-adjustment, the General once more got up to permit that to be done, and stepping over to the cot near by, fell over it, weak and weary. Then Henry observing that the atmosphere of the room was very close, proposed that the chairs should be drawn into the parlor for the General's occupancy there.

This was accordingly done, and then the Colonel on one side, and Henry on the other, conducted the General back into the parlor, and he was seated again there.

At this moment I returned to the cottage, having been absent for a few moments. I found that with this increase of weakness, there was a slight rise in temperature, and greater frequency of pulse.

Later, the General intimated that he wanted writing materials. A pad and pencil were brought him, and a writing board put over the arms of his chair.

He wrote something to the Colonel, who upon reading it, replied: "That has already been attended to, father."

Telegrams were sent to U. S. Grant, Jr. and to the consulting surgeons, summoning them by earliest train.

About 10 o'clock, hearing the voices of some members of his family upon the piazza, he whispered to me "Tell them to retire. I wish no one to be disturbed on my account."

Col. Grant, Henry and myself remained with him. The rest of the family, obeying the General's expressed wish, retired to their own rooms.

During the night, hypodermics of brandy were given, which temporarily steadied the flickering pulse, and apparently revived the General. No stimulants were given by the mouth. He was perfectly conscious, responding by movement whenever addressed, and seemed cognizant of everything that was occurring about him, and to be awaiting with perfect composure, the final change which he knew was near at hand.

During this period of revival, he wrote two messages, both of which were immediately given to Col. Grant.

The last one was addressed to me, but I do not know the tenor, considering that these last messages should belong strictly to the family, whatever they might be.

July 22. Wednesday.

The night passed without any great change in the situation. Early this morning, the General took a part of a tumbler of milk, the most he has taken at any time since yesterday. The day is warm, and the expectancy gloomy.

During the morning, in answer to his repeated solicitation for the hypodermic of morphine, I had given him at times two or three minims largely diluted with water.

At one time he wrote me this morning, which is the last writing I have: "I do not think I slept the last time because of the medicine, which put me to sleep the first and second time, so much as from a general breaking up of my loss of sleep. I think I had better try it once more."

At 12 o'clock, the clock striking eleven, and his chair being so situated that he could see its face, he wrote to the Colonel: "Fix the clock right. It only struck eleven."

At 3 P.M., Drs. Sands and Shrady arrived, and at the same time Mr. and Mrs. U. S. Grant Jr., who immediately went in to see the General.

His family were now all with him, and he greeted his son Ulysses with an intelligent look, and a slight movement of the lips, as though he wanted to speak.

The consulting surgeons came in later, looked at him, and saw that professional aid was no longer of any avail.

At 7 P.M., while I was seated at the dinner table at the hotel, Harrison came for me, saying that the General had suddenly become weaker. I immediately hastened to the cottage, and found that the General had been transferred from the chair in which a few moments before I had left him seated, to the bed, which had been hastily prepared for him, and was then lying on his back, a position I had not seen him occupy at any time during his sickness.

His pulse was much weaker and faster, and his weakness was evidently rapidly increasing.

I immediately repeated the hypodermic of brandy, and waited. There was a slight revival, and in ten minutes I again repeated the hypodermic of brandy.

Soon after this, both Dr. Sands and Dr. Shrady came down from the hotel, and we all recognized that the end was very near.

Every one about the cottage remained up, expecting the end at any moment.

As the hours drew on, the symptoms of dissolution grew. The respiration quickened, the pulse became small and very frequent, the limbs finally became cold, the respiration shallower and quicker, the pulse too frequent to be counted.

The brain was alive to the last moment. Occasionally during the night, there were evidences of his appreciation of the presence of those about him. At one time he was asked if he was in pain, to which he distinctly replied, "No!"

Again he was asked if he wanted anything, to which he answered "Water."

Henry kept his mouth constantly moist. Hot applications were applied to his feet, and mustard to his stomach. Brandy was occasionally administered hypodermically, not with expectation of benefit, but to relieve possible distress.

The action of the heart ran up from 80 rapidly to 100, and by degrees higher, until it could not be counted; his respiration from 20 a minute, to 30 and 40 and even 60.

At sunrise I walked up to the brow of the hill in front of the hotel, just as the first rays of the new day shot over the summit of the mountains in the East, and illuminated the valley upon which the General had looked when he took the ride only three days before.

After standing there a few moments, looking at the sunrise, and breathing in the pure and delicious air of the early morning, I returned to the cottage and resumed my place among the watchers.

Going to the bedside, I found the General's respiration had notably increased in frequency during my short absence; the rhythm of the heart had become so rapid and irregular that the pulse could not be counted, the impulse too had become so weak that venuous stagnation had taken place; the blue discoloration about the nails presaging approaching dissolution.

The respiration continued, becoming shorter and shallower. Yet there was no expression of pain or suffering of any kind.

In this state, hour after hour passed. There was so much of peace and quiet in the attitude, that most of the members of the family went to their rooms, to catch a few moments of repose in expectation of another day of watching. Henry remained vigilant.

About seven, Dr. Sands having come down from the hotel,

Dr. Shrady and myself met him upon the piazza, and while we were then discussing the situation, Henry came hurriedly out from the parlor, and said that a sudden change had come over the General's features; he thought he was dying.

I immediately went in, and confirmed this opinion by my own observations, and sent Henry at once to summon such members of the family as were temporarily absent. In a moment they were all there.

Having resigned my chair to Mrs. Grant—she sat there, holding the General's hand in hers, and looking earnestly into his face. When Col. Grant came in, Henry gave him his place near the General and the Colonel passed his left arm under his father's head, so as partially to sustain it as Henry had done.

Mrs. Sartoris stood immediately behind her mother.

Near her, and at the foot of the bed, stood Mr. and Mrs. U. S. Grant, Jr., next Mrs. F. D. Grant, then Mrs. Jesse R. Grant, and near to her, around the corner of the bed, Mr. J. R. Grant. I stood a little behind Mrs. Genl. Grant, and between her and the Colonel, watch in hand, observing every change.

Behind this group in the room, stood Drs. Sands and Shrady together. Henry, when he gave up his place at the General's head to the Colonel, retired to the door leading out on to the veranda. Harrison came in from the chamber, and stood in the embrasure of the chimney.

The breathing each instant became feebler and feebler, and soon ceased altogether.

There was no expiring sigh. Life passed away so quietly, so peacefully, that, to be sure it had terminated, we waited a minute. Then looking at my watch, I found it was precisely eight.

The exhaustion following the excursion to the Eastern Outlook had been sudden and complete.

Now the watching was over; the efforts to prolong life were at an end. Through these efforts the General had been spared much pain, and many disagreeable features of the disease. His strength had been sustained and his intellect kept unclouded, and he had been enabled to accomplish his great desire, the completion of his Memoirs.

Notes

Chapter 1: General Grant Becomes an Author

1. Adam Badeau, *Grant in Peace. From Appomattox to Mount Mc-Gregor. A Personal Memoir* (Hartford, 1887), p. 316; Major General Ulysses S. Grant 3rd, *Ulysses S. Grant: Warrior and Statesman* (New York, 1969), p. 380.
2. U. S. Grant 3rd, *Ulysses S. Grant: Warrior and Statesman,* pp. 426–27.
3. A. Badeau, "The Last Days of General Grant," *Century Magazine,* Vol. 30, n.s. Vol. 8 (October 1885) p. 920; U. S. Grant 3rd, *Ulysses S. Grant: Warrior and Statesman,* p. 427.
4. Ulysses S. Grant, William M. Evarts, and Joseph W. Drexel to George Jones, January 1884, George E. Jones Papers, New York Public Library.
5. Badeau, *Grant in Peace,* pp. 349, 391–95; *New York Times,* May 7, 1880.
6. *Times,* September 25, October 14, November 12, 1880, April 26, May 24, 1881; *Laws of the State of New York,* 1881, Vol. 1, Chap. 36; *Trow's Business Directory of New York City,* 1882, pp. 40, 677; "The General's Last Victory," *New York State and The Civil War* 2 (August 1962): 3.
7. Badeau, *Grant in Peace,* pp. 351–53, 395–97; "The Railway Invasion of Mexico," *Harper's Magazine* 65 (October 1882): 745; *Congressional Record,* 48th Cong., 1st Sess., 5261, 2d Sess., 1042, 1059; *Times,* October 14, 1882, January 23, 1883, June 11, 1885; *New York Tribune,* January 19–20, March 12, 14, 1884.
8. Badeau, "The Last Days of General Grant," p. 920; *Tribune,* May 7, 1884; New York *Sun,* May 7, 11, 1884.
9. *Times,* May 7, 1884; *Tribune,* May 7, 1884; *Sun,* May 15, 1884; Henry Clews, *Twenty-eight Years in Wall Street* (New York, 1888), pp. 160–70.
10. *Times,* May 8–13, 15, 21, July 8, 1884; *Tribune,* May 8, 13, 1884.

11. *Times,* May 14, 1884; Clews, *Twenty-eight Years in Wall Street,* pp. 36–37.
12. *Sun,* May 13, 27–28, 1884; *Tribune,* May 26–28, 1884; Clews, *Twenty-eight Years in Wall Street,* pp. 219–21.
13. Badeau, "The Last Days of General Grant," 921; *Times,* January 12, 1885.
14. *Times,* December 30–31, 1884, January 12, February 4, 1885; *Tribune,* December 10, 28, 1884, January 8, 13, 1885; New York *World,* January 4, 1885.
15. *Times,* June 18, 1884; Hamlin Garland, "A Romance of Wall Street: The Grant and Ward Failure," *McClure's Magazine* 10 (April 1898): 505; Clews, *Twenty-eight Years in Wall Street,* p. 215.
16. *Tribune,* June 23, 1886.
17. *Times,* November 12, 1880, March 18, 1881; *Sun,* May 16, 1884; Grant Fund Letters, 1880–86, George E. Jones Papers.
18. Robert U. Johnson, *Remembered Yesterdays* (Boston, 1923), p. 209; Badeau, *Grant in Peace,* 554–55.
19. Badeau, *Grant in Peace,* pp. 559–60; Johnson, *Remembered Yesterdays,* p. 210; *Times,* June 12, 1884; Richard Watson Gilder to Robert U. Johnson, June 13, 1884; Robert Underwood Johnson Papers, Manuscripts and Archives Division, The New York Public Library, Astor, Lenox and Tilden Foundations.
20. Johnson, *Remembered Yesterdays,* pp. 210–13.
21. Gilder to Johnson, July 1, 1884, Johnson Papers; Clarence C. Buel to Gilder, July 1, 1884, Richard Watson Gilder Papers, Manuscripts and Archives Division, The New York Public Library, Astor, Lenox and Tilden Foundations; Johnson to Gilder, July 1, 1884, ibid.
22. Johnson, *Remembered Yesterdays,* pp. 213–15.
23. Ibid., pp. 215–16.
24. Gilder to Roswell Smith, July 3, 1884, Johnson Papers; Smith to Gilder, July 8, 1884, Gilder Papers; Gilder to Johnson, Buel et al., July 21, 1884, Johnson Papers; Johnson to Gilder, July 22, 1884, Gilder Papers.
25. *Times,* July 27, 1884, quoting the *Baltimore American;* Gilder to Johnson, July 28, 1884, Johnson Papers.
26. Gilder to Johnson, August 18, 1884, Johnson Papers; Buel to Johnson, August 20, 1884, ibid.
27. Johnson to Buel, August 19, 1884, Johnson Papers; F. H. Scott to Johnson, August 20, 1884, ibid.; Johnson to Buel, August 21, 1884, ibid.; Buel to Smith, August 24, 1884, ibid.; Smith to Gilder, August 24, 1884, Gilder Papers.
28. Gilder to Smith, August 27, August 29, 1884, Johnson Papers.
29. Johnson, *Remembered Yesterdays,* pp. 216–17; Smith to Gilder, September 9, 1884, Gilder Papers.

30. Gilder to Johnson, September 10, 1884, Johnson Papers; Badeau, *Grant in Peace,* pp. 563–64.
31. *Dictionary of American Biography,* s.v. "Badeau, Adam."
32. Badeau, *Grant in Peace,* p. 560; Johnson, *Remembered Yesterdays,* pp. 215–16; *Times,* July 27, 1884.
33. Badeau, *Grant in Peace,* pp. 560–62; Johnson, *Remembered Yesterdays,* pp. 215–16; Johnson to Gilder, July 22, 1884, Gilder Papers.
34. Badeau, *Grant in Peace,* pp. 564–65.
35. Albert B. Paine, *Mark Twain, A Biography: The Personal and Literary Life of Samuel Langhorne Clemens,* 3 vols. (New York, 1912), 2:711–13.
36. Samuel L. Clemens, *Mark Twain's Autobiography,* 2 vols. (New York, 1924), 1:32–33; Hamlin Hill. ed., *Mark Twain's Letters to his Publishers, 1867–1894* (Berkeley, 1967), pp. 177–78.
37. Paine, *Mark Twain,* 2:799–800; Hill, *Mark Twain's Letters to his Publishers,* p. 185; Rosamond Gilder, ed., *Letters of Richard Watson Gilder* (Boston, 1916), p. 123.
38. Paine, *Mark Twain,* 2:801–2; Clemens, *Mark Twain's Autobiography,* 1:33–36.
39. Clemens, *Mark Twain's Autobiography,* 1:37–39; Paine, *Mark Twain,* 2:802–3; Samuel C. Webster, ed., *Mark Twain, Business Man* (Boston, 1946), pp. 299, 302.
40. Clemens, *Mark Twain's Autobiography,* 1:48; Paine, *Mark Twain,* 2:803.
41. *World,* March 9, 1885; Johnson, *Remembered Yesterdays,* pp. 217–18; Clemens, *Mark Twain's Autobiography,* 1:38–39, 54.
42. Paine, *Mark Twain,* 2:803–4; *World,* February 20, 1885.

Chapter 2: The General Is Stricken

1. *Times,* August 18, 1882, quoting the *Denver News; Times,* December 28, 1883; Badeau, "The Last Days of General Grant," pp. 919, 921.
2. O. P. Clarke, *General Grant at Mount MacGregor* (Saratoga Springs, 1906), p. 9; George W. Childs, *Recollections of General Grant* (Philadelphia, 1885), pp. 20–21.
3. Childs, *Recollections of General Grant,* p. 21; Horace Green, *General Grant's Last Stand: A Biography* (New York, 1936), pp. 282–84.
4. Green, *General Grant's Last Stand: A Biography,* pp. 286–87; Badeau, "The Last Days of General Grant," pp. 922–23.
5. Green, *General Grant's Last Stand: A Biography,* pp. 287–88; *Times,* December 29, 1884.
6. *Times,* January 12, 1885; M. J. Cramer, *Ulysses S. Grant; Conversations and Unpublished Letters* (New York, 1897), pp. 175–76.

7. *World,* February 4, 1885; *Tribune,* July 23, 1885.
8. *World,* February 20, 28, 1885; *Times,* March 1, 1885.
9. Paine, *Mark Twain,* 2:803–6; Clemens, *Mark Twain's Autobiography,* 1:48.
10. *World,* March 1, 1885.
11. Childs, *Recollections of General Grant,* pp. 30–31; Clemens, *Mark Twain's Autobiography,* 1:40–42; Paine, *Mark Twain,* 2:807; Albert Bigelow Paine, ed., *Mark Twain's Letters,* 2 vols. (New York, 1917), 2:451.
12. Webster, *Mark Twain, Business Man,* p. 305; Paine, *Mark Twain,* 2:805–6.
13. Hill, *Mark Twain's Letters to his Publishers,* pp. 184–85.
14. G. F. Shrady, "General Grant's Last Days," *Century Magazine* 76 (May–July 1908): 102–4, 416; Hamlin Garland, "Ulysses Grant —His Last Year," *McClure's Magazine* 11 (May 1898): 89–90; *Times,* March 13, 1885.
15. Paine, *Mark Twain,* 2:807–9.
16. *Tribune,* March 21, 27, 1885; *Times,* March 25–28, 1885.
17. *Times,* March 29–31, April 1–3, 1885; *Tribune,* April 3, 1885; Shrady, "General Grant's Last Days," pp. 416–17; Stefan Lorant, "The Baptism of U.S. Grant," *Life,* March 26, 1951, pp. 92–93.
18. Shrady, "General Grant's Last Days," p. 413.
19. *Times,* April 8–9, 12, 15, 17, 1885; *World,* April 8–9, 15, 17–18, 1885.
20. *Times,* April 28, 1885; Green, *General Grant's Last Stand: A Biography,* p. 303; Badeau, "The Last Days of General Grant," pp. 931, 934–36.
21. Webster, *Mark Twain, Business Man,* pp. 316–17; Paine, *Mark Twain,* 2:809–10. Webster thought later that dictation had improved Grant's style. *Times,* October 13, 1885.
22. *World,* April 29, 1885.
23. *Tribune,* April 30, May 1, 1885; *Sun,* May 1, 1885; *World,* May 1, 1885; Webster, *Mark Twain, Business Man,* p. 319.
24. *Tribune,* May 6, 1885; *Sun,* May 6–7, 1885.
25. Paine, *Mark Twain,* 2:810; *New York Herald,* March 17, 1888; Bruce Catton, "U. S. Grant: Man of Letters," *American Heritage* 19 (June 1968): 97–98.
26. *Herald,* March 17, 1888; Catton, "U. S. Grant: Man of Letters," pp. 97–98.
27. *Herald,* March 17, 21, 1888.
28. Ibid., March 21, 1888. Mrs. Grant finally paid Badeau, the affair being settled without a trial. *Tribune,* October 31, 1888.
29. Green, *General Grant's Last Stand: A Biography,* p. 305; Henry Nash Smith and William M. Gibson, eds., *Mark Twain—Howells*

Letters: The Correspondence of Samuel L. Clemens and William D. Howells, 1872–1910, 2 vols. (Cambridge, Mass., 1960), 2:528–29; *Tribune,* May 6, 8–10, 12–16, 1885; *Times,* May 18, 20, 1885.

30. *Times,* May 21, 1885; *Tribune,* May 23, 1885; Paine, *Mark Twain,* 2:811–12.

31. *Times,* June 3, 1885.

32. Ibid., June 9, 1885; Paine, *Mark Twain's Letters,* 2:462. Before he left New York, Grant suggested to his son that, if he should not be able to do any more work, Francis Vinton Greene, whose study of the Mississippi campaigns of the Civil War had appeared in 1883, be employed to help in the final editing. U. S. Grant to Fred Grant, June 15, 1885, Francis Vinton Greene Papers, New York Public Library.

Chapter 3: Mount McGregor Becomes a Summer Resort

1. George B. Anderson, *Our County and Its People: a Descriptive and Biographical Record of Saratoga County, New York,* 2 vols. (Boston, 1899), 1:391–92.

2. Ibid., pp. 133–34.

3. *Appletons' Illustrated Hand-Book of American Travel* (New York, 1857), pp. 149–50.

4. New England–New York Inter-Agency Committee, "Historical Data for Report of the Recreation Study and Report Group on Sub-Region 'C,' " mimeographed (Boston, 1954), pp. 25–26.

5. Ibid., p. 27.

6. J. A. Holden, *Glens Falls, New York, "The Empire City"; Our Part and Place in History* (Glens Falls, 1908), p. 7; O. P. Clarke, *General Grant at Mount MacGregor,* p. 5; *Mt. McGregor, the Popular Summer Sanitarium, Forty Minutes from Saratoga Springs* (Buffalo, 1884), pp. 5–6.

7. Martha J. Clarke, "General Grant and Mount MacGregor," Grant Cottage Records, Mount McGregor, Wilton, N. Y.; Rev. Robert G. Adams to Edna Steere Newton, September 28, 1915, ibid.; Nathaniel B. Sylvester, *History of Saratoga County, New York* (Philadelphia, 1878), pp. 463, 469. Mrs. Clarke gives 1872 as the date of completion of the hotel, but this is clearly much too early.

8. *Mt. McGregor, the Popular Summer Sanitarium, Forty Minutes from Saratoga Springs,* pp. 7–8; *Times,* June 29, 1885.

9. Washington Frothingham, ed., *History of Montgomery County* (Syracuse, 1892), pp. 259–60, and ibid., Pt. 2, "Family Sketches," p. 1; George R. Howell and J. Tenney, eds., *Bi-Centennial History of Albany: History of the County of Albany, N. Y., from 1609 to*

1886 (New York, 1886), p. 377; "The General's Last Victory," *New York State and the Civil War* 2 (August 1962): 13.

10. W. J. Arkell, *Old Friends and Some Acquaintances* (Los Angeles, 1927), pp. 49–50.
11. Anderson, *Our County and Its People,* 1:181; *Mt. McGregor, the Popular Summer Sanitarium, Forty Minutes from Saratoga Springs,* pp. 8–9.
12. Deed Book 161, pp. 268–76, February 1–3, 1883, Office of the County Clerk, Saratoga County; *Laws of the State of New York,* 1850, Chap. 140; ibid., 1883, Chap. 41.
13. O. P. Clarke, *General Grant at Mount MacGregor,* p. 7; Martha J. Clarke, "General Grant and Mount MacGregor."
14. *Catalogue of the Mount McGregor Art Association, 1883* (Albany, 1883), passim.
15. *Benedict's Diary, Local Events from "Daily Saratogian" and "Saratoga Daily Journal" 1875–1896* (Saratoga Springs, 1897?), entry for February 1884; *Mt. McGregor, the Popular Summer Sanitarium, Forty Minutes from Saratoga Springs,* pp. 9–10.
16. *Mt. McGregor, the Popular Summer Sanitarium, Forty Minutes from Saratoga Springs,* pp. 10–12.
17. Ibid., pp. 14–15, 19–23.
18. Ibid., pp. 25–27.
19. Nathaniel B. Sylvester, *The Historic Muse on Mount McGregor, One of the Adirondacks, Near Saratoga* (Troy, 1885), pp. 9, 23.
20. O. P. Clarke, *General Grant at Mount MacGregor,* p. 7.
21. *Times,* March 26, 1888.
22. Evelyn B. Britten (Jean McGregor, pseud.), *Chronicles of Saratoga. A Series of Articles Published by the "Saratogian," Saratoga Springs, New York* (Saratoga Springs, 1947), pp. 98–99; Martha J. Clarke, "General Grant and Mount MacGregor"; *Times,* July 24, 1885.
23. *World,* June 17, 1885. There were only two engines, later named *John Brill* and *Henry Denton.* Martha J. Clarke, "General Grant and Mount MacGregor."
24. *Times,* June 16, 21, 1885.

Chapter 4: Last Days at Mount McGregor

1. Shrady, "General Grant's Last Days," p. 419; Arkell, *Old Friends and Some Acquaintances,* p. 50; O. P. Clarke, *General Grant at Mount MacGregor,* p. 7.
2. *World,* July 12, 1885; U. S. Grant, William M. Evarts, and Joseph W. Drexel to George Jones, January 1884, George E. Jones Papers.
3. "The Last Days of General Grant," *Harper's Weekly,* August 15,

1885, p. 538; Deed Book 183, p. 518, April 1, 1885, and Deed Book 184, p. 250, April 1, 1885, Office of the County Clerk, Saratoga County.

4. *Tribune,* April 19, 26, 1885; *World,* April 21, 1885.
5. O. P. Clarke, *General Grant at Mount MacGregor,* pp. 11–12, quoting the *Albany Evening Journal,* June 16, 1885.
6. *Times,* June 12, 1885, quoting the *Commercial Advertiser.*
7. Ibid.
8. *Tribune,* June 15, 1885.
9. O. P. Clarke, *General Grant at Mount MacGregor,* pp. 7–8; *New York Evening Post,* June 15, 1885; *World,* June 15, 1885.
10. *World,* June 16, 1885; *Times,* June 16, 1885.
11. *Commercial Advertiser,* June 16, 1885; *Times,* June 17, 1885; *Tribune,* June 17, 1885; *World,* June 17, 1885.
12. *World,* June 17, 1885.
13. Ibid.; *Times,* June 17, 1885.
14. *Herald,* June 17, 1885; *Tribune,* June 17, 1885.
15. *Herald,* June 18, 1885; *World,* June 18, 1885; Garland, "Ulysses Grant—His Last Year," p. 93; Horace Green, "General Grant's Last Stand," *Harper's Magazine* 170 (April 1935): 536–37.
16. *Times,* June 18–19, 1885; *Tribune,* June 19, 1885.
17. Ishbel Ross, *The General's Wife: The Life of Mrs. Ulysses S. Grant* (New York, 1959), p. 304.
18. Bruce Catton, "Two Porches, Two Parades," *American Heritage* 17 (June 1966): 65; *Times,* June 22, 1885.
19. *Times,* June 20, 23, 1885.
20. *World,* June 17, 1885; *Herald,* June 20–22, 1885; *Evening Post,* June 20, 1885; *Times,* June 22, 1885; *Tribune,* June 22–23, 1885.
21. *Times,* June 21, 1885; *Sun,* June 21, 1885; *Tribune,* June 22, 1885.
22. Green, "General Grant's Last Stand," 537; *Times,* June 24, 1885; *Tribune,* June 24–25, 1885; *Herald,* June 24, 1885.
23. *Times,* June 24–25, 1885.
24. Shrady, "General Grant's Last Days," p. 423.
25. *Tribune,* June 26, 1885; *Times,* June 26, 1885.
26. *Times,* June 27, 1885.
27. Ibid., June 28, 1885; *Herald,* June 28, 1885; *World,* June 28, 1885; Green, "General Grant's Last Stand," p. 537.
28. Ross, *The General's Wife,* pp. 304–5.
29. Ibid., p. 305; *Evening Post,* June 18–19, 1885.
30. *Times,* June 29, 1885.
31. Paine, *Mark Twain,* 2:813–14.
32. Ibid., p. 814.
33. *Sun,* July 2, 1885; *Evening Post,* July 3, 1885.
34. *Commercial Advertiser,* July 3, 1885.

35. Clemens, *Mark Twain's Autobiography,* 1:68–70; Lorant, "Baptism of U. S. Grant," pp. 98, 101. Grant's refusal to take communion is recorded in an undated note to Dr. Newman among the Grant manuscripts at the United States Military Academy Library, West Point.

36. *Times,* July 2–3, 1885. As the book was later published, there were three short chapters and a conclusion following the account of Appomattox. Ulysses S. Grant, *Personal Memoirs of U. S. Grant,* 2 vols. (New York, 1885–86), Vol. 2, Chaps. 68–70 and Conclusion. All of this material, amounting to 56 printed pages, seems to have been written at Mount McGregor.

37. *Tribune,* July 7–8, 1885.

38. Grant Family Papers, Courtesy of the daughters of the late Maj. Gen. U. S. Grant 3rd.

39. Badeau, "The Last Days of General Grant," p. 937.

40. Webster, *Mark Twain, Business Man,* pp. 314–15; *Times,* July 24, August 20, 1885.

41. *Times,* July 4, 1885; *Tribune,* July 5, 1885.

42. *Tribune,* July 6, 1885; *Times,* July 6, 1885; *Herald,* July 6, 1885.

43. *Times,* July 7–8, 1885; *Herald,* July 7–8, 1885; *Tribune,* July 8, 1885; *Evening Post,* July 7, 1885; Green, "General Grant's Last Stand," p. 538.

44. *Times,* July 9, 1885; *World,* July 9, 1885; *Herald,* July 9, 1885; Garland, "Ulysses Grant—His Last Year," p. 94.

45. U. S. Grant to "My Dearest Wife," July 8, 1885, Grant Family Papers.

46. *Times,* July 10, 1885; *Herald,* July 10, 1885; Johnson, *Remembered Yesterdays,* p. 223.

47. *World,* March 1, 1885; Clemens, *Mark Twain's Autobiography,* 1:49–53; Hill, *Mark Twain's Letters to his Publishers,* p. 185; Johnson to Buel, June 29–30, July 1–2, 8, 12, 1885, Johnson Papers.

48. Johnson, *Remembered Yesterdays,* pp. 219, 223–24. The abbreviated article on Vicksburg appeared in *Century Magazine,* September 1885, three months before the appearance of the first volume of the *Personal Memoirs.* Grant's article on the Wilderness was never completed.

49. *Times,* July 11, 16, 1885; *Herald,* July 11, 1885; Garland, "Ulysses Grant—His Last Year," p. 95.

50. Ross, *The General's Wife,* pp. 307–8; Green, "General Grant's Last Stand," p. 539.

51. *Commercial Advertiser,* July 11, 1885.

52. *Times,* July 24, 1885.

53. *Herald,* July 12, 1885; Ross, *The General's Wife,* p. 308; U. S. Grant to Fred Grant, n.d., Grant Family Papers.

54. *Times,* July 12–14, 1885; *Tribune,* July 13, 1885; *World,* July 14, 1885.
55. *Herald,* July 14–15, 1885; *Sun,* July 14, 1885.
56. *Times,* July 17, 1885; *Herald,* July 17, 1885; Green, "General Grant's Last Stand," p. 539.
57. *Times,* July 18–20, 1885; *Evening Post,* July 17, 1885; *Herald,* July 18–19, 1885.
58. Shrady, "General Grant's Last Days," p. 427.
59. *Times,* July 20, 1885; *Tribune,* July 20, 1885; *Herald,* July 20, 1885; Green, *General Grant's Last Stand: A Biography,* p. 309. T. C. Crawford, a special correspondent for the New York *World,* who spent some time at Mount McGregor, says that Grant continued writing on the *Memoirs,* "completing the last chapter of twelve thousand words only four days before he died." T. C. Crawford, "General Grant's Greatest Year," *McClure's Magazine* 2 (May 1894): 538–39. Bruce Catton says that "Grant died just two days after he had written his final words." Catton, "U. S. Grant: Man of Letters," p. 99. The evidence is that anything that Grant may have written on the book after July 11 was highly fragmentary. His last effort, made against doctors' orders, seems to have been on July 13.
60. *Times,* July 21, 1885.
61. Ibid., July 22, 1885, *World,* July 22, 1885.
62. *Tribune,* July 22, 1885.
63. *Times,* July 23, 1885; Mrs. F. D. Grant to Mrs. O. P. Clarke, December 6, 1923, Grant Cottage Records.
64. *Times,* July 24, 1885; *Herald,* July 24, 1885; O. P. Clarke, *General Grant at Mount MacGregor,* pp. 45–46; Ross, *The General's Wife,* pp. 310–11.
65. Paine, *Mark Twain,* 2:815.

Chapter 5: The General Leaves the Mountain

1. "The Death of General Grant," *Frank Leslie's Illustrated Newspaper,* August 1, 1885, p. 383; "The General's Last Victory," p. 19; *World,* July 24, 1885; *Herald,* August 1, 1885; Johnson to Buel, July 22, 1885, Johnson Papers; Samuel L. Clemens to Karl Gerhardt, June 4, 1885, Miscellaneous S. L. Clemens Manuscripts, The New-York Historical Society. There was an unpleasant dispute over the ownership of the death mask later. Mrs. Grant wanted it, but Gerhardt held out for an outrageous price. Mark Twain undertook to get it away from him for her. Webster, *Mark Twain, Business Man,* pp. 343–46.
2. *Tribune,* July 24–25, 1885; *World,* July 24, 26, 1885. The story circulated later that Douglas had called Holmes, the Saratoga under-

taker, and Dr. Newman had taken it upon himself to send for Merritt, who took charge on his arrival, Douglas and Holmes withdrawing gracefully. There had long been friction between Douglas and Newman. *Commercial Advertiser,* July 30, 1885. Other accounts indicate that Colonel Fred had called Merritt.

3. *World,* July 24, 1885; *Times,* July 25, 27, 1885.
4. *Times,* July 24, 1885; *Tribune,* July 25, 1885; *World,* July 24, 1885.
5. *Times,* July 25, 1885; *Tribune,* July 28–29, 1885; *Evening Post,* July 27, 1885.
6. *Times,* July 25, 1885; *Tribune,* July 25, 1885.
7. *Tribune,* July 24, 1885, quoting the Charleston *News and Courier; Herald,* July 25, 1885.
8. Paine, *Mark Twain,* 2:815; Ross, *The General's Wife,* p. 312.
9. *Times,* July 25, 1885.
10. *Tribune,* July 26, 1885; *Herald,* July 29, 1885.
11. *World,* July 24, 1885; *Tribune,* July 25, 1885.
12. *World,* July 24, 1885; *Herald,* July 26–28, 1885. Drexel's title to the cottage was not confirmed until the deed was "sealed and delivered" on September 17.
13. *Evening Post,* July 24, 1885.
14. *Tribune,* July 27, 1885.
15. *Times,* July 28, 1885; *Tribune,* July 28, 1885.
16. *Tribune,* July 27, 1885; *Times,* July 28–29, August 2, 1885.
17. *Times,* July 25, 1885; *Tribune,* July 30, 1885.
18. *Times,* July 31, 1885; Crawford, "General Grant's Greatest Year," p. 537.
19. *Times,* July 31, 1885; *Tribune,* July 31, 1885.
20. *Times,* August 1, 1885.
21. Ibid., August 2, 1885. Further bleaching and coloring were applied later, however. Ibid., August 3, 1885.
22. *Times,* July 3, 31, August 1–2, 1885; *World,* July 31, 1885; Ross, *The General's Wife,* p. 307. Mrs. Ross says that the cottage was struck on July 4, apparently drawing on the rather confused childhood recollections of Ulysses S. Grant 3rd. July 4 was his birthday, as well as that of his aunt Nellie. "The flash grazed small Ulysses and knocked him off his feet."
23. *World,* August 2, 1885; "The Honored Dead," *Frank Leslie's Illustrated Newspaper,* August 8, 1885, p. 403.
24. *Times,* August 3, 1885; *Tribune,* August 3, 1885.
25. *Times,* August 4, 1885; *Tribune,* August 4, 1885.
26. *Times,* August 4, 1885.
27. Ibid., August 5, 1885; *Tribune,* August 5, 1885.
28. *Tribune,* August 5, 1885; *Times,* August 5, 1885; *Benedict's Diary,* entry for August 4, 1885.

29. *Times,* August 6–9, 1885; *Tribune,* August 9, 1885.
30. Ross, *The General's Wife,* pp. 313–16.
31. *Times,* July 26, August 10, 1885; *Tribune,* August 11, 1885.
32. *Times,* August 17, 1885, quoting the *Philadelphia Press.*
33. *Times,* August 22, 1885.
34. *Benedict's Diary,* entry for August 31, 1885; Fred Grant to Joseph W. Drexel, August 29, 1885, Lucy W. Drexel, comp., "Francis' Old New York," Folio edition, Vol. X (The New-York Historical Society), p. 83; Princess Cantacuzene, Countess Speransky, née Grant, *My Life Here and There* (New York, 1921), pp. 58–59; *Tribune,* September 14, 1885. Colonel Grant seems to have spent most of his time at Mount McGregor acknowledging letters of condolence. F. D. Grant to Hamilton Fish, Mount McGregor, August 28, 1885, Ulysses S. Grant Papers, Library of Congress.
35. Paine, *Mark Twain's Letters,* 2:457–60.
36. Paine, *Mark Twain,* 2:816; Hill, *Mark Twain's Letters to his Publishers,* pp. 191–95; Webster, *Mark Twain, Business Man,* p. 348; *Times,* May 10, 1886. The material taken from the manuscript of the *Personal Memoirs* that Colonel Grant sold to the *North American Review* involved two Lincoln anecdotes. It appeared not in the magazine itself but in Allen Thorndike Rice, ed., *Reminiscences of Abraham Lincoln by Distinguished Men of his Time* (New York, 1886), pp. 1–4.
37. Paine, *Mark Twain,* 2:816; *Tribune,* February 28, 1886.
38. *Tribune,* December 2, 1885; Catton, "U. S. Grant: Man of Letters," p. 99; Edmund Wilson, "Books: Homage to General Grant," *New Yorker,* April 4, 1953, p. 119.

Chapter 6: The Cottage Becomes a Shrine

1. *Times,* July 24–25, 1885; *Herald,* July 26, 1885.
2. *Times,* August 3, 1885.
3. *Congressional Record,* 49th Cong., 1st Sess., 2885; *Times,* June 7, 1886.
4. *Times,* July 31, August 13, 1887.
5. Grand Army of the Republic, *Journal of the National Encampment,* 1887 (Milwaukee, 1888), p. 35; Grand Army of the Republic, Department of New York, *Abstract of General Orders and Proceedings of Annual Encampments,* 1894 (Albany, 1894), pp. 98–99; *Times,* March 26, April 10, 1888.
6. G.A.R., N. Y., *Abstract of General Orders,* 1889, pp. 62–63; O. P. Clarke, *General Grant at Mount MacGregor,* p. 8; *Laws of the State of New York,* 1889, Chap. 5.
7. G.A.R., N. Y., *Abstract of General Orders,* 1890, pp. 54–55; Martha

J. Clarke, "General Grant and Mount MacGregor"; *Benedict's Diary,* entry for November 2, 1889.

8. G.A.R., N. Y., *Abstract of General Orders,* 1890, pp. 55–56; Martha J. Clarke, "General Grant and Mount MacGregor."

9. G.A.R., N. Y., *Abstract of General Orders,* 1891, pp. 147–48.

10. Ibid., 1893, pp. 102–4, 257–58.

11. Ibid., 1894, pp. 98–103.

12. Ibid., 1895, pp. 104, 279–80.

13. Ibid., 1896, pp. 114–16; *Laws of the State of New York,* 1896, Chap. 667.

14. *Laws of the State of New York,* 1897, Chap. 790.

15. Anderson, *Our County and its People,* 1:181–82; Britten, *Chronicles of Saratoga,* p. 100; O. P. Clarke, *General Grant at Mount Mac-Gregor,* p. 5; Arkell, *Old Friends and Some Acquaintances,* pp. 50–51.

16. *Laws of the State of New York,* 1900, Chaps. 418, 419; ibid., 1905, Vol. 2, Chaps. 699, 700; *Annual Report of the American Scenic and Historic Preservation Society,* 1908 (Albany, 1908), pp. 54–56.

17. *Visitors' and Automobilists' Guide Book and Maps of Saratoga Springs and Vicinity* (Saratoga Springs, 1910), pp. 58–60.

18. Martha J. Clarke, "General Grant and Mount MacGregor," postscript by Mrs. A. J. Gambino.

19. *Annual Report of the American Scenic and Historic Preservation Society,* 1924, p. 47; *Laws of the State of New York,* 1957, Vol. 2, Chap. 420.

20. Louis I. Dublin, *A 40-Year Campaign Against Tuberculosis* (New York, 1952), pp. 4–14, 19–22, 35–36.

21. Ibid., pp. 14, 35–36; *Times,* March 1, August 6, 1946, April 23, June 7, 14, 24, October 13, 1957, July 24, December 17, 27, 1959, February 2, 13, April 11, 1960.

Bibliographical Note

GRANT MANUSCRIPTS for the final year of the general's life are scattered and unaccountably thin. There are very few letters of this period in the principal collection, the Ulysses S. Grant Papers, at the Library of Congress. This collection does include the manuscript of the *Personal Memoirs of U. S. Grant,* as far as it was drafted by the general and not dictated. The manuscript is in his distinctive hand, leaving no question of authorship, though there are interlineations and revisions in more than one hand, as might be expected.

The John Hancock Douglas Papers in the Library of Congress contain many handwritten notes from Grant to his principal physician, and a typescript copy of an immensely detailed diary, replete with clinical detail, entitled "Records of the Last Days of the Magnanimous Soldier U. S. Grant." Both diary and notes have been drawn upon heavily by Douglas's nephew, Horace Green, in an article and a book on Grant's final days.

The Grant family has some of the notes written by the general in his last days to his wife Julia and his son Fred. (Copies of these Grant Family Papers were graciously made available for this study by the daughters of the late Maj. Gen. U. S. Grant 3rd.) A few notes written by the general to the Reverend Dr. John P. Newman at Mount McGregor are among the Grant manuscripts at the United States Military Academy Library, West Point.

The New York Public Library Manuscripts and Archives Division has the papers of Richard Watson Gilder and Robert Underwood Johnson, containing much valuable material on the preparation of the articles that Grant wrote for the *Century Magazine,* the germ of the *Personal Memoirs,* and on the book project itself. Also in the

153

New York Public Library are the George E. Jones Papers, with detail on the fund raised for Grant's benefit in 1880–81, and one interesting letter signed by the general and others in 1884. One Grant letter of 1885, bearing on the completion of the *Memoirs*, is in the Francis Vinton Greene Papers.

The New-York Historical Society has several letters written by Colonel Fred Grant from Mount McGregor to Mr. and Mrs. Joseph W. Drexel in appreciation of their hospitality to the general and his family. These are in a folio of miscellaneous material assembled by Lucy W. Drexel covering events, chiefly in New York City, related to the Drexels during the period 1872–92. This volume was recently acquired by the society and is catalogued as "Francis' Old New York," Folio edition, Vol. X. Also in the New-York Historical Society is a letter from Samuel L. Clemens to Karl Gerhardt, the sculptor, accounting for the latter's presence on Mount McGregor when the general died.

There is useful manuscript material among the records at the Grant cottage on Mount McGregor, including a number of letters by members of the Grant family and others in answer to questions raised about events on the mountain and at the cottage, especially in 1885. There is also an unpaged manuscript by Martha J. Clarke, custodian of the cottage from 1917 to 1941, covering the development of the Mount McGregor resort, Grant's stay at the cottage, and later events on the mountain. No papers of W. J. Arkell, promoter of Mount McGregor, or Joseph W. Drexel, his associate, except as noted above, have been located. Records in the Office of the County Clerk, Saratoga County, Ballston Spa, N. Y., include deed books and other material relating to the ownership of Mount McGregor and the Drexel (Grant) cottage.

Published documents found helpful in this study include the annual volumes of *Laws of the State of New York,* which include special legislation relating to the development of Mount McGregor and the administration of the Grant cottage after the general's death. In this latter connection, the annual volumes published by the Grand Army of the Republic, Department of New York, *Abstract of General Orders and Proceedings of Annual Encampments,* have been most useful. The *Annual Report of the American Scenic and Historic Preservation Society* for 1908 has an excellent brief description of the cottage, and there is further material on it in the 1924 report of this organization. The *Catalogue of the Mount McGregor Art Association, 1883* (Albany, 1883) is an interesting item describing an enterprise on the mountain that promised much but faded quickly.

Heavy reliance has been placed on newspaper material. Grant's final illness, death, and funeral formed the biggest continuing news story of 1885, and the amount of coverage devoted to it is staggering. New York metropolitan journals have been drawn on pretty much in the order of their accessibility. The *New York Times* and the *New York Tribune* are both indexed for the whole period, and complete files are readily available. These have been used very extensively. The New York *World* also has an index for the year 1885 and this was found very useful. Other New York newspapers drawn on include the *Commercial Advertiser, Herald, Evening Post,* and *Sun.*

A good many periodical articles have been written on General Grant in his last days, beginning chronologically with A. Badeau, "The Last Days of General Grant," *Century Magazine,* Vol. 30, n.s. Vol. 8 (October 1885). Badeau was already preparing an article on Grant for the *Century* when the general died. T. C. Crawford, one of the reporters at Mount McGregor in 1885, is the author of "General Grant's Greatest Year," *McClure's Magazine* 2 (May 1894). Hamlin Garland wrote two articles on Grant's final year, later incorporated in a biography: "A Romance of Wall Street: The Grant and Ward Failure," *McClure's Magazine* 10 (April 1898), and "Ulysses Grant—His Last Year," *McClure's Magazine* 11 (May 1898). Dr. George F. Shrady summed up the clinical aspects of Grant's case in a long article, "The Surgical and Pathological Aspects of General Grant's Case," for the *Medical Record,* August 1, 1885, which was also printed in full in the *New York Tribune,* July 31, 1885. Shrady toward the end of his life also wrote a continued article with emphasis on the medical side of Grant's illness, but nontechnical and highly readable, "General Grant's Last Days," *Century Magazine* 76 (May–July 1908). This material appeared in book form a little later. Horace Green covered the same ground, using primarily Dr. Douglas's papers, in "General Grant's Last Stand," *Harper's Magazine* 170 (April 1935). Stefan Lorant discovered the diary kept by the Reverend Dr. John P. Newman during his ministrations to the dying general, and prepared from it a brief article, "The Baptism of U. S. Grant," *Life,* March 26, 1951. A well-informed, unsigned article on General Grant at Mount McGregor is "The General's Last Victory," *New York State and the Civil War* 2 (August 1962). Bruce Catton, who has written two volumes of what promises to be the definitive biography of Grant, has done two brief articles referring to the last period of Grant's life: "Two Porches, Two Parades," *American Heritage* 17 (June 1966), and "U. S. Grant: Man of Letters," *American Heritage* 19 (June 1968).

Biographies of Grant are numerous and vary widely in quality. Some of them cover only his early years and Civil War service. Others concentrate on his presidency. A number of quick-sale biographies, most of them without great merit, appeared immediately after Grant's death, recounting briefly the story of his last days. Adam Badeau, who had written a three-volume work on Grant's military career, began working on a sequel before the general died, and two years later published *Grant in Peace. From Appomattox to Mount McGregor. A Personal Memoir* (Hartford, 1887). While it stresses the intimacy of Badeau's relations with Grant, it contains much material not found elsewhere. George W. Childs, Grant's neighbor at Long Branch, wrote a chapter of personal reminiscences for one of the 1885 Grant biographies, and also published it separately as *Recollections of General Grant* (Philadelphia, 1885). It has interesting detail on the general's life at Long Branch, including the beginning of his fatal illness. Oliver P. Clarke, custodian of the Grant cottage at Mount McGregor, produced a little volume, entitled *General Grant at Mount McGregor* (Saratoga Springs, 1906), based largely on source material. M. J. Cramer, *Ulysses S. Grant; Conversations and Unpublished Letters* (New York, 1897), has some letters from Grant to his sister, Mrs. Cramer, including an interesting one from the period of his illness. Dr. Shrady's *General Grant's Last Days* (New York, 1908) is practically a reprint of his article on the same subject. Hamlin Garland's *Ulysses S. Grant, His Life and Character* (New York, 1898), one of the better biographies, uses his earlier articles for his concluding chapter. Horace Green's *General Grant's Last Stand: A Biography* (New York, 1936) merely fleshes out his periodical articles with slight earlier material and adds a few unpublished photographs. The best scholarly work on Grant in recent years has concentrated on his earlier career. Major General Ulysses S. Grant 3rd, *Ulysses S. Grant: Warrior and Statesman* (New York, 1969), is disappointingly thin on the final phase of his grandfather's life, but has some material drawn from family records and traditions not readily available in other form.

A charming biography of Mrs. Grant, evidently based on extensive access to family papers, is Ishbel Ross, *The General's Wife: The Life of Mrs. Ulysses S. Grant* (New York, 1959). It has a good bit of information on life in the Grant household during the general's last year. Grant's granddaughter Julia, who was nine at the time of the general's death, spent the summer of 1885 at the cottage on Mount McGregor and later moved back to the house in New York with her parents. Her memoirs, Princess Cantacuzene, Countess Speransky, née Grant, *My Life Here and There* (New York, 1921), have fleeting glimpses of events in both places.

Mark Twain, whose firm published Grant's *Personal Memoirs,* has received almost as much biographical attention as the general. The official biography, Albert Bigelow Paine, *Mark Twain, A Biography: The Personal and Literary Life of Samuel Langhorne Clemens,* 3 vols. (New York, 1912), has considerable detail on Twain's friendship with Grant and on the preparation and publication of the general's book. Other works by or about Twain found to contain material valuable for the present study include Samuel L. Clemens, *Mark Twain's Autobiography,* 2 vols. (New York, 1924), which has contemporary material not found in Paine's biography. Other studies on Twain that yield fresh material include Albert Bigelow Paine, ed., *Mark Twain's Letters,* 2 vols. (New York, 1917); Hamlin Hill, ed., *Mark Twain's Letters to his Publishers, 1867–1894* (Berkeley, 1967); Henry Nash Smith and William M. Gibson, eds., *Mark Twain—Howells Letters: The Correspondence of Samuel L. Clemens and William Dean Howells, 1872–1910,* 2 vols. (Cambridge, Mass., 1960); and Samuel C. Webster, ed., *Mark Twain, Business Man* (Boston, 1946).

W. J. Arkell, *Old Friends and Some Acquaintances* (Los Angeles, 1927), being the reminiscences of the promoter of Mount McGregor as a summer resort, has illuminating material on the circumstances under which General Grant was taken to the mountain in 1885, and on the general history of the area. Henry Clews, *Twenty-eight Years in Wall Street* (New York, 1888), has interesting sidelights on the failure of Grant & Ward in 1884. The beginnings of Grant's literary activity are traced in broad strokes in Robert U. Johnson, *Remembered Yesterdays* (Boston, 1923). Some further material on this topic is found in Rosamond Gilder, ed., *Letters of Richard Watson Gilder* (Boston, 1916).

Local history has been drawn on for the story of Mount McGregor. Useful material has been found in a number of local works.

George B. Anderson, *Our County and its People: a Descriptive and Biographical Record of Saratoga County, New York,* 2 vols. (Boston, 1899), has good background information on Saratoga Springs and Mount McGregor. *Benedict's Diary, Local Events from "Daily Saratogian" and "Saratoga Daily Journal" 1875–1896* (Saratoga Springs, 1897?), has a few dated events relating to Mount McGregor not found elsewhere. Evelyn B. Britten (Jean McGregor, pseud.), *Chronicles of Saratoga. A Series of Articles Published by the "Saratogian," Saratoga Springs, New York* (Saratoga Springs, 1947), has material on the Drexel family at Saratoga and on the Hotel Balmoral at Mount McGregor. Louis I. Dublin, *A 40-year Campaign Against Tuberculosis* (New York, 1952), has much detail on the sanitarium established by the Metropolitan Life Insurance Company on Mount McGregor in 1913. Cornelius E. Durkee, comp., *Reminiscences of Saratoga* (Saratoga Springs, 1928), has a few facts on Mount McGregor not found elsewhere. Washington Frothingham, ed., *History of Montgomery County* (Syracuse, 1892), has information on W. J. Arkell of Canajoharie and his family. J. A. Holden, *Glens Falls, New York, "The Empire City": Our Part and Place in History* (Glens Falls, 1908), has a few facts on Duncan McGregor. George R. Howell and J. Tenney, eds., *Bi-Centennial History of Albany: History of the County of Albany, N. Y., from 1609 to 1886* (New York, 1886), records the fact that W. J. Arkell, his father, and Joseph W. Drexel were in business together as proprietors of the *Albany Evening Journal* at the time of Grant's stay on Mount McGregor. An advertising brochure of the time, *Mt. McGregor, the Popular Summer Sanitarium, Forty Minutes from Saratoga Springs* (Buffalo, 1884), has a detailed description of the resort in the year before Grant came there. Nathaniel B. Sylvester, *History of Saratoga County, New York* (Philadelphia, 1878), tells of Duncan McGregor's efforts to develop the mountain named for him. The same author's *The Historic Muse on Mount McGregor, One of the Adirondacks, Near Saratoga* (Troy, 1885), is a brief history of the mountain with a lyrical description of its attractions for the summer visitor to Saratoga Springs. The *Visitors' and Automobilists' Guide Book and Maps of Saratoga Springs and Vicinity* (Saratoga Springs, 1910), describes Mount McGregor and the Grant cottage as they were at the time, urging tourists to visit them.

Index

159